Social Sustainability, Resilience and Community Urban Development

Urban communities around the world face increased stress from natural disasters linked to climate change, and other urban pressures. They need to grow rapidly stronger in order to cope, adapt and flourish. Strong social networks and social cohesion can be more important for a community's resilience than the actual physical structures of a city. But how can urban planning and design support these critical collective social strengths?

This book offers blue sky thinking from the applied social and behavioural sciences, and urban planning. It looks at case studies from 14 countries around the world – including India, the USA, South Africa, Indonesia, the UK and New Zealand – focusing on initiatives for housing, public space and transport stops, and also natural disasters such as flooding and earthquakes. Building on these insights, the authors propose a 'gold standard': a socially aware planning process and policy recommendation for those drawing up city sustainability and climate change resilience strategies, and urban developers looking to build climate-proof infrastructure and spaces.

This book will be of great interest to students and scholars of urban studies, resilience studies and climate change policy, as well as policy-makers and practitioners working in related fields.

Cathy Baldwin is an Applied Social and Behavioural Scientist and Public Health Consultant, Research Associate at the University of Oxford, and Visiting Researcher at Oxford Brookes University, UK.

Robin King is Director of Knowledge Capture and Collaboration at the World Resources Institute (WRI), and Adjunct Professor, Georgetown University, USA.

Endorsements

'The authors advocate for the importance of social planning and design through a variety of international case studies that demonstrate community resilience. They contend that traditional planning approaches often overlook the significance of social sustainability, which is the basic ingredient for the health and well-being of communities. This collection provides valuable insights for architects, planners, policy makers, community leaders, and students.'

Henry Sanoff, Professor Emeritus of Architecture,
North Carolina State University, USA

'This timely and creative book links the usually separated fields of urban resilience and community resilience with community resilience, sustainability and social justice. It encourages planners, and those who shape their own settlements, to find ways of supporting the social processes that underpin community resilience, through the idea of "socially aware planning".'

Helen Ross, The School of Agriculture and Food Sciences,
The University of Queensland, Australia

'As the world becomes increasingly urban, planners, politicians, and social scientists increasingly direct their attention to the challenges of urban development, social sustainability, and community resilience. As they do so, we increasingly categorize urban life economically, sociologically, and anthropologically. Development, sustainability, and resilience become nouns – objects to be studied, dissected, and debated. Baldwin and King's informative volume reminds us that they are verbs; actions which are never completed. In doing so they rediscover how people should stand at the center of our attention when we think about our necessarily urban future.'

Blair A. Ruble, Woodrow Wilson Center, Washington, USA

Routledge Focus on Environment and Sustainability

The Application of Science in Environmental Impact Assessment
By Aaron Mackinnon, Peter Duinker and Tony Walker

Jainism and Environmental Philosophy
Karma and the Web of Life
By Aidan Rankin

Social Sustainability, Climate Resilience and Community-Based Urban Development
What About the People?
By Cathy Baldwin and Robin King

Social Sustainability, Climate Resilience and Community-Based Urban Development

What About the People?

Cathy Baldwin and Robin King

LONDON AND NEW YORK

First published 2018 by Routledge

2 Park Square, Milton Park, Abingdon, Oxfordshire OX14 4RN

52 Vanderbilt Avenue, New York, NY 10017

Routledge is an imprint of the Taylor & Francis Group, an informa business

First issued in paperback 2020

British Library Cataloguing in Publication Data
A catalogue record for this book is available from the British Library

Library of Congress Cataloging in Publication Data
Names: Baldwin, Cathy, 1976- author. | King, Robin (Sociologist) author.
Title: Social Sustainability, Climate Resilience and Community-Based
Urban Development : What About the People? / Cathy Baldwin and Robin
King.Description: 1 Edition. | New York : Routledge, 2018. |Series:
Routledge focus on environment and sustainability | Includes
bibliographical references and index.Identifiers: LCCN 2018004104|ISBN
9781138478015 (hardback : alk. paper) | ISBN 9781351103329
(ebook)Subjects: LCSH: Sociology, Urban. | Cities and towns–Growth. |
City planning–Environmental aspects. | Community development.
Classification: LCC HT151 .B2655 2018 | DDC 307.76–dc23LC record
available at https://lccn.loc.gov/2018004104

ISBN 13: 978-1-138-47801-5 (hbk)
ISBN 13: 978-0-367-45902-4 (pbk)

Typeset in Times New Roman
by Swales & Willis Ltd, Exeter, Devon, UK

To our friends and families who keep us cheerful

Contents

Figures

Tables

Preface

The Preface introduces the research that forms the basis of this book. It can be read as an Executive Summary of the book and outlines the broad background to the project: the current planetary crisis of global warming and climate change that the book is responding to; the main arguments about connecting daily *urban social sustainability* and intermittent *climate-resilience in urban communities*; the major theories used in the book's analytical framework; the 21 featured case studies across issues of *social sustainability* and *community resilience*; the methodologies used; a summary of results and of the *four-stage socially aware planning process* that the book advocates to urban development stakeholders; and an overview of which chapters offer special interest content to different readers.

This book was conceived, researched and written at the World Resources Institute (WRI), Washington DC, USA during 2013–2014 and afterwards as a transatlantic collaboration between the authors. Two preliminary articles were published online on *The City Fix*, WRI's urban development and sustainable transport blog, one outlining our research in February 2014: http://thecityfix.com/blog/new-approach-social-factors-urban-development-cathy-baldwin/ and a second unveiling a draft in June 2017: http://thecityfix.com/blog/what-about-the-people-unlocking-the-key-to-socially-sustainable-and-resilient-communities-cathy-baldwin-robin-king/

With a steady global increase in urban stressors, and the effects of global warming and climate change such as adverse weather events and natural disasters, urban communities worldwide need to grow stronger rapidly. This book was prompted by a disheartening myopia in some political, policy and planning quarters as to how humanity should adapt to, and cope with this biggest planetary crisis facing civilisation, a force for uncertain futures. Ironically, powerful humans propose technological and economic measures to address the problem of resilience, yet neglect the potential power of resilient acts among their own kind, despite growing interest.

Strong networks and social cohesion mean that communities and the individuals that constitute them are better able to cooperate and take actions to support each other. In addition to the services and support provided by formal authorities, people who feel invested in the place where they live may be more likely to care for it, and be motivated to act when it is affected by a negative environment event. The book explores the relationship between urban built environments and 'pro-community' behaviours and psychological responses: positive acts and states of mind beneficial to communities and their constituent individuals. Its context is both urban development projects and frameworks (15) and natural disaster contexts (5) in 14 countries in the global north and south. Its core argument is that built environments planned, designed, built, located, and managed with social interaction in mind can support pro-community behaviours that contribute to daily social sustainability, and help strengthen resilience to unplanned environmental adversities.

Social sustainability is concerned with communities' health, well-being and quality of life, and their capacity to function effectively in future. Community resilience is about communities developing the adaptive capacity to cope during, and adapt after natural disasters. At local neighbourhood level, both ideas are underpinned by social capital and social cohesion, (sometimes) positive social and psychosocial processes where residents are drawn to cooperate in networks, get along in spite of differences, and think and feel positively about or fondly of the people among whom they reside, and the places where they live. Most pro-community behaviours and states of mind can trace a relationship to social capital or social cohesion as a composite theoretical dimension, or an outcome in the social and psychological sciences. Consequently, daily social sustainability and intermittent community resilience sit on a single continuum, linked together by connected and shared pro-community behaviours and states of mind.

The book takes up the term 'socially aware planning' to describe the intention to influence pro-community behaviours and create positive social impacts via a development plan, resulting in a 'socially planned built environment'. It analyses how in the public and private sector, and community co-created building and development projects with explicit socially aware planning goals for the construction/regeneration of housing, public space and transport stops, urban form and public participation influenced existing and potential residents' pro-community behaviours. These analyses are presented as qualitative case studies from the following cities and regions: Delhi (India) – public usage of public open spaces;

Cape Town (South Africa) – upgrading of unsafe walkways and public spaces in an informal settlement, and redesign of the Central railway station; Belfast (Northern Ireland, UK) – a planned private-developer housing complex; southern England (UK) – private-developer housing communities; Portland, Oregon (USA) – volunteer renovation of public squares; Manchester (England, UK) – volunteer renovation of a small public green space; Christchurch (New Zealand) – planned upgrade of the city's Bus Xchange; Yala (Thailand) – new city parks and green spaces, and Buenos Aires (Argentina) – a public campaign to maintain a supportive historic neighbourhood environment.

Seven theoretical pro-community behaviours and states of mind were tested on eight case studies (the Buenos Aires and Yala cases did not contain sufficient behavioural data but are included as useful illustrative examples) and confirmed, and five new ones uncovered. The authors draw on literature from both urban planning and the social and psychological sciences in an attempt to combine approaches that are often divorced from each other, but through their synthesis offer new insights. Case studies are offered on policy frameworks from Vancouver, Canada, Adelaide, Australia, and a multi-city example from UNESCO. An example from Paraguay shows how social capital and cohesion help a community to collectively maintain their infrastructure. An example from Rio de Janeiro, Brazil, shows how social and physical resources for social sustainability and resilience have developed organically within the informal *favela* communities.

The book then examines six case studies exploring the relationships between the built environment/social infrastructure, and existing or lacking social organisational strategies grounded in pro-community behaviours that hindered or promoted behavioural resilience during and after· disasters in cities. Some of the socially sustainable pro-community behaviours and other similar ones enabled urban residents to cope with, and adapt to, adverse impacts on their communities/built structures. Case studies are offered as follows: three concerned with coping during/after flooding: two in Surat (India), and one in Jakarta (Indonesia); coping during/after ongoing episodes of intense heat, rain and flooding events, cyclones and storm surges: Khulna (Bangladesh); coping after Hurricane Katrina: New Orleans, Louisiana (USA); and after earthquakes: Christchurch (New Zealand). Six theoretical pro-community behaviours and states of mind were tested and confirmed (and one physical one), and 11 new ones uncovered (alongside additional physical and community infrastructural ones).

These analyses revealed nine shared pro-community behavioural and psychological dimensions of a community that is both socially sustainable and resilient. These are: connections and affective attachments to the neighbourhood and community (pride in, sense of, or attachment to place/community; sense of belonging); social interactions with neighbours/in the neighbourhood; feelings of safety and security, and active monitoring; residential stability; proactive participation in collective group/civic activities and affairs; social cohesion; social solidarity/community spirit; happiness and well-being; and voice and influence, and civic empowerment. All the pro-community behaviours and states of mind tested and uncovered in the book are open to planner and designer influence.

The urban development projects reviewed enhanced social sustainability through influencing pro-community behaviours by: incorporating clear social objectives into planning; adopting multiple strategies for social research – to understand the local interpretation of the urban landscape, and produce evidence of communities' social needs, resources and 'strengths' (the specific local dimensions of 'resources'), employing democratic and inclusive community participation and engagement with professional stakeholders; matching these data with sensitive planning and design decisions; allowing communities to co-design, implement and participate in managing projects, especially their own spaces and infrastructure, thereby growing social bonds, collective capacity and other social resources with positive social, health and well-being effects; creating off-shoot community and economic development opportunities; and conducting ongoing monitoring and evaluation using various methods to include communities, ensure social objectives are honoured, and generate learning to better inform future plans.

In the community resilience cases, poor quality and vulnerably located built structures, poverty, weak networks and lack of cohesion within heterogeneous settlements, and lack of participation/influence in formal resilience planning inhibited behavioural resilience in informal settlements. An ongoing challenge is to ensure that communities at all income levels have access to appropriate materials and structures to promote resilience. The informal and formal built environment was partially responsible for the development of social capital and cohesion in residential communities, resources that were then drawn upon in micro-level coping and adaptation strategies employed to manage the effects of disasters. Communal open-air spaces facilitated social networking, trust and sense of community, but exposed residents to climate hazards unless protective physical features were installed. Built environments were used flexibly to support community gatherings. Participating in urban planning and collective maintenance of an urban environment with higher income, long-term residents prior to an adversity improved participation and resilience afterwards. Women's community leadership, economic empowerment, and climate-proofed homes, social and business spaces were achieved when women gained voice and influence in settlement design and upgrading initiatives. Separating people's key social networks from their usual built environments and accommodating them in problematic temporary structures produced negative social and health effects.

Insights from analysis of the case studies suggested that development stakeholders should adopt four stages of a socially aware planning process that incorporates principles from a Social or Health impact assessment (SIA and HIA). The process begins from a scheme's earliest conception, then follows the entire development. Stage 1, *Scheme Conception and Real Estate Pre-Development,* leads on to Stage 2, *Research and Community Engagement.* The social and cultural data, in addition to more traditional economic and financial data, explicitly inform the *Design and Implementation* decisions of Stage 3, and Stage 4, *Monitoring and Evaluation,* closes the loop and provides information for future construction as well as improvements. The book closes with a set of recommendations encompassing ideas, tools and methods to guide urban development stakeholders wanting to construct or regenerate built environments that support pro-community behaviours using the 'socially aware planning' approach. These emphasise the importance of equity, diversity and community involvement and co-design. They can be read as a stand-alone guide for urban development stakeholders seeking implementation advice, rather than the conceptual background of our research. For those with specific interests, please refer to the following Chapters:

Theoretical framework on urban social sustainability: 3 and 4.

Theoretical framework on urban community resilience: 5.

Qualitative case studies on socially sustainable built environment initiatives: 6 and 7.

The four stages of a socially aware planning process for urban development stakeholders: 7.

Qualitative case studies on resilient neighbourhood communities: 8.

Behaviours and psychological responses indicative of the socially sustainable, resilient community open to planner and designer manipulation: 9.

Conclusion: 9.

Recommendations: 10

Acknowledgements

This book resulted from Cathy's time at the World Resources Institute (WRI) in Washington DC as a Postdoctoral Associate in Anthropology, University of Oxford. Good fortune brought her to Robin, to whom heartfelt thanks are due; thanks also to Marcus Banks, Robert Parkin and the staff of the Institute of Social and Cultural Anthropology, University of Oxford, and Bridget Durning of Oxford Brookes University for continued institutional support.

Grateful thanks to: Samantha Burch, Janice Y. Ho, Catalina Angel, Thomas Abbot and Hansa Srinivasan, WRI interns summer 2014, for helping locate case study materials; Jude Ball, Ben Cave, Breeda McGrath, Tye McMahon, Blair Ruble and Saffron Woodcraft for kindly commenting on our draft; Jamie Anderson, Matt Bell, Lucia Caistor-Arendar, Huraera Jabeen, Will Norman, Sadasivam Karuppannan, Lubaina Rangwala, Jan Semenza, Alpana Sivam, Arnold Spokane, Mario Wilhelm and Saffron Woodcraft for feedback on case studies as source author or reviewer; Hugh Pryor for graphic layouts; and Shirley Baldwin.

Glossary

Contextual and core concepts

Urban development: This term is used in different ways in different communities. From Collins Dictionary: the development or improvement of an urban area by building; an urban area that has been developed and improved by building. A more academic definition: Urban development is the social, cultural, economic and physical development of cities, as well as the underlying causes of these processes (Dept of Sociology and Human Geography, University of Oslo, 2011). Our definition: the process by which cities develop physically, economically, socially and culturally, as well as the result and a place in which such development occurs.

Built environment: Human created and constructed space where people live and interact (our definition).

Community: Groups or networks of people who share a common sense of belonging based on shared connections such as geographic proximity, interests, socio-demographic characteristics, experiences, emotional links or other common purposes. Communities may be based on face-to-face interactions or virtual or mental connections that bind them; they can emerge informally or be formally organised. The term 'community' is also used to describe: organised networks, policy discourses, or group identities (our definition).

Neighbourhood: A place-based area or district, especially one forming a section of a town or city, that generates neighbourly or identity-based feeling and behaviour, often leading to a sense of community (our definition).

Social organisation: The ways in which people organise themselves in a society or community to live together and meet their social needs; it includes arrangements for forming and conducting relationships, the roles people play, the rules and codes of conduct, and the goals and

...comes of those relationships that result in key social activities and the functionality of the society or community (our definition).

ocial sustainability: Social sustainability is about people's quality of life, now and in the future. It describes the extent to which a neighbourhood supports individual and collective well-being. Social sustainability combines design of the physical environment with a focus on how the people who live in and use a space relate to each other and function as a community (Woodcraft, 2012: 35).

Community resilience: Community resilience is the existence, development and engagement of community resources by community members to thrive in an environment characterised by change, uncertainty, unpredictability and surprise. Members of resilient communities intentionally develop personal and collective capacity that they engage with to respond to and influence change, to sustain and renew the community, and to develop new trajectories for the communities' future (Magis, 2010: 402).

Adaptive capacity: 'The capability of a particular system to effectively cope with shocks' (Martin-Breen and Marty Anderies, 2011: 14).

Economic sustainability: The maintenance of economic capital (Goodland, 1995).

Environmental sustainability (sometimes also referred to as physical sustainability, or natural resource sustainability): Protecting natural resources, often referred to as natural capital, over the long run, and our ability to access them responsibly to support present and future generations. Resilience refers to the ability to bounce back (EPA, n.d., citing the US National Environmental Policy Act of 1969).

Social capital and social cohesion

Social capital: The behavioural norms, trust, and reciprocity that help people to form social networks for the purpose of collective cooperation and mutual benefits (based on the work of Bourdieu, 1985; Coleman, 1988a and b and 1990; Portes, 1998; Putnam, 1993 and 2000).

Cognitive social capital: Cognitive (mental) attributes that people share such as behavioural norms, trust, reciprocity, values, attitudes and beliefs (Coutts et al. 2007; Uphoff, 2000; Grootaert and van Bastelaer, 2001).

Structural social capital: The ways that people organise themselves together on a social level through structures such as social networks, patterns of civic engagement, and established roles (Grootaert and van Bastelaer, 2001; Uphoff, 2000; Coutts et al., 2007).

Bonding social capital: Social capital between people who share characteristics in common such as family members, neighbours, close friends and colleagues (homogeneous social groups) (Grootaert and van Bastelaer, 2001; Coutts et al., 2007).

Bridging social capital: Social capital between groups of people who have very different characteristics from each other, such as age, gender, ethnicity, socio-economic status, religion, disability, language (heterogeneous social groups) (Grootaert and van Bastelaer, 2001; Coutts et al., 2007).

Horizontal social capital: Social capital that links people who have equal or near equal status in a hierarchy (Grootaert and van Bastelaer, 2001; Coutts et al., 2007).

Vertical (or Linking) social capital: Social capital linking groups of people to powerful institutions, or linking them to people with different levels of status, resources or power (Coutts et al., 2007; OECD, 2001).

Social cohesion: When people from the same community or society get along, trust each other, and live peacefully together with or without social or ethnic differences. This is supported by economic equality and inclusion, democracy, people having their basic needs met, and social solidarity (our definition based on the work of Berger-Schmitt, 2000; Forrest and Kearns, 2001; Ferroni, Mateo and Payne, 2008; Jenson, 2010).

Concepts describing life standards

Human capital: The skills, knowledge, capacity to work, and good health that together enable people to pursue different livelihood strategies and achieve their livelihood outcomes. At a household level, human capital is a factor of the amount and quantity of labour available. This varies according to household size, skill level, education, leadership potential, health status etc. Human capital is necessary to be able to make use of the other four types of livelihood assets (DFID, 1999).

Quality of life: A term used widely in different contexts, and highly subjective and self-defined, with both positive and negative elements. In general, it refers to well-being of an individual (our definition).

Well-being: Well-being relates to the state of being or doing well in life, being happy, healthy, or prosperous (The OECD, 2001), as a broad and encompassing concept 'that takes into consideration the whole person. Beyond specific physical and/or psychological symptoms related to health, well-being should include context-free measures of life experiences' (e.g. life satisfaction, happiness) (Danna and Griffin, 1999: 364).

Behavourial and mental well-being concepts

Behaviour: Individual and group human actions.

Psychological response: All forms of mental response to human experiences.

Pro-community behaviours: 'A broad category of acts that are beneficial to the community at large as well as to other community residents' (Oishi *et al.*, 2007: 831).

Psychosocial: 'Pertaining to the influence of social factors on an individual's mind or behaviour and to the interrelation of behavioural and social factors' (Oxford English Dictionary cited in Martikainen, Bartley, & Lahelma, 2002: 1091).

Social support: 'Resources provided by other persons' (Cohen and Syme, 1985) and 'information leading the subject to believe he is cared for and loved, is esteemed and valued and belongs to a social network of communication and mutual obligation' (Cobb, 1976).

Concepts describing the workings of society and community

Social infrastructure: The total of organisations, services, and social relationships that facilitate coexistence in fairness (neighbourhoods, groups, networks and families) and participation in society (Engbersen and Sprinkhuizen, 1997). A distinction is made between formal infrastructure which refers to those services and arrangements available in a neighbourhood or town that stimulate the social climate (a sports club or community centre), and the informal infrastructure which refers to social networks that exist in a specific neighbourhood (Konig, 2002: 79).

Social equity: 'Equal opportunity, in a safe and healthy environment' (United States President's Council on Sustainable Development, 1996).

Social integration: 'The ability of different groups in society to live together in productive and cooperative harmony and to accommodate differences within a framework of common interest to the benefit of all. Social integration implies justice for the individual and harmony among different social groups and countries. It means integration of disadvantaged and vulnerable groups by making all institutions of society more accessible to them' (Vanclay *et al.*, 2015).

Social inclusion: The process and outcome of improving the terms for individuals and groups to take part in society (World Bank, 2013).

Social exclusion: A process and outcome where individuals and groups are excluded from actively participating in, and benefiting from, society's activities and opportunities (our definition).

Social order: 'The conditions under which individuals and groups are prepared to co-operate with one another to reach common goals' (Wrong, 1994).

Social attributes and occurrences

Social resources: Attributes within the social environment (e.g. social capital, social cohesion, social connectedness, social equity, social inclusion etc.) that social groups (e.g. communities, ethnic groups etc.) can engage with or draw upon to their individual and collective advantage (our definition).

Social strengths: The locally specific social conditions, organisational forms, relationships, psychosocial attachments and identifications, cognitive features, collective abilities, and other social capital- and cohesion-related attributes that people can draw upon to achieve social objectives and benefits (our definition).

Social process: An intangible social occurrence taking place in a society or community where people interact and engage with external factors that result in social outcomes either in isolated or ongoing fashion. For example, the formation and negotiation of social capital or increase or decrease in social cohesion. Most social processes include the formation (and maintenance, or not) of individual and group relationships, what people accomplish within them, and changes to such patterns of social activity (our definition; cf. Gillin and Gillin, 1954).

Social change processes: Categories of social change processes include demographic, economic, geographic institutional and legal, emancipatory and empowerment, sociocultural and others. These are set in motion by projects or policies and take place independently of the social context, leading to social impacts (adapted from Vanclay, 2002: 193).

Social impacts: Social consequences to human populations of public or private actions which change the ways in which people live, work, play, relate to one another, organise to meet their needs and cope as members of society. Social impacts must be experienced or felt (adapted from Vanclay, 2002: 190).

Cultural impacts: Changes to the behavioural norms, values and beliefs of people that guide and rationalise their cognition of themselves and their society (adapted from Vanclay, 2002: 190).

Health impacts: A health impact can be positive or negative. A positive health impact is an effect that contributes to good health or to improving health. A negative health impact has the opposite effect, causing or contributing to ill health (adapted from: WHO website, Health Impact Assessment, Glossary of Terms used, http://www.who.int/hia/about/glos/en/).

Social outcomes: The longer-term results of a change process, e.g. social change, urban development etc. (our definition).

Social benefits: When a project activity or process contributes an effect (social benefit) that improves the existing baseline social conditions through identifying needs and proposing actions to help address them (adapted from Rowan and Streather, 2011: 219).

Psychosocial orientations and attachments to place and community[1]

Orientations

Place orientation: A generalised 'personal orientation to place' (Hummon, 1992: 262) that rests on 'awareness of one's location in the environment' and psychological familiarity (cf. La Grow, 2010).

Sense of place: An individual's personal connection to and sensory experience of a built or biophysical place as understood through the meanings given to its characteristics. It encompasses personal positive, neutral or negative regard for it, developed psychologically through prolonged or repeated exposure to the place (cf. Hummon, 1992: 262; Trentelman, 2009: 201; Williams and Kitchen, 2012: 258).

Sense of community: An individual's personal feeling of being recognised and included in a community as based on their experience of membership (cf. Hyde and Chavis, 2007: 179) and component factors identified by the individual.

Social solidarity and community spirit: A feeling of unity and togetherness, and a tendency to act together with other members of a social group (e.g. a community, ethnic group etc) in its collective interest (our definition)

Attachments

Place attachment: The environmental settings to which people are 'emotionally and culturally attached' (Low and Altman, 1992: 5) to varying degrees (Williams and Vaske, 2003: 832) in a positive sense. Attachments to places are developed through interaction with them or experience of them regularly and over time, or through story-telling about and memory of them (Trentelman, 2009: 200).

Community attachment: A measure of an individual's emotional attachment to their community and indicator of their rootedness within it (Trentelman, 2009: 201), arising from interactions and connections with fellow community members (Kasarda and Janowitz 1974: 328). It generally contributes to positive individual well-being through the benefits of social connection and social support and information provision by extensive networks (Lee and Blanchard, 2012: 25; 28).

Sense of belonging: An individual's 'naturalised emotional attachment' (Yuval-Davis, 2006: 197; 199) to a group of people, organisation, biophysical or socio-cultural environment, formed psychologically through social interaction with and within groups, organisations and environments (cf. Hagerty *et al.*, 1992: 173). People are more likely to become conscious of to whom, what and where they belong when their belonging is questioned or threatened.

Relevant forms of impact assessments

Social impact assessment (SIA): Includes the processes of analysing, monitoring and managing the intended and unintended social consequences, both positive and negative, of planned interventions (policies, programmes, plans, projects) and any social change processes invoked by those interventions. Its primary purpose is to bring about a more sustainable and equitable biophysical and human environment (Vanclay *et al.*, 2015).

Health impact assessment (HIA): A combination of procedures, methods and tools that systematically judges the potential, and sometimes unintended, effects of a policy, plan, programme or project on both the health of a population and the distribution of those effects within the population. HIA identifies appropriate actions to manage those effects (Quigley *et al.*, 2006).

Note

1 Original formulations from Baldwin, 2015.

1 Context and rationale

This book unites three major strands of cities research and policy of interest to governments, planners, designers, architects, social scientists and others: Urban Development, Social Sustainability and Community (Social)[1] Resilience, to the impacts of global warming and climate change. It explores the influence of urban planning, design and the development of urban built environments on residents'/users' *pro-community behaviours* (including psychological states of mind) in 14 countries, through urban form and public participation. The psychological term 'pro-community behaviours' is defined as: 'a broad category of acts that are beneficial to the community at large as well as to other community residents' (Oishi *et al.*, 2007: 831). Urban social networks of residents or 'communities' need to develop their capacity for pro-community action more urgently than ever due to climate change. Pro-community behaviours and psychological responses are at the root of the daily social sustainability of communities in 'normal' times, and their resilience to the negative impacts of unplanned adverse environmental events and natural disasters. The urban sector can contribute to the development of capacity for pro-community behaviours by creating built environments that encourage and support them. We use the term 'socially aware planning'[2] to describe the intention to influence such behaviours and create positive social impacts via the development process, with the resulting product being a 'socially planned built environment'.

Built environments planned with social awareness are imperative. The 3.5 billion people living in the world's urban centres (Thwaites, 2015) face numerous pressures and challenges. Urban residents make up more than half the earth's population (United Nations, n.d.) with 4.9 billion – about 60 per cent of total global population – expected to live in cities by 2030 (Global Commission on the Climate and Economy, 2014: 60; United Nations, 2005; WHO, n.d.). Astoundingly, 60 per cent of the area expected to be urban by 2030 – predominantly in Asia and Africa –

has not been constructed yet (Thwaites, 2015). Rapid urbanisation due to economic growth and population expansion puts pressure on available land, urban infrastructure, and green space worldwide. It is occurring faster than governments or markets can provide safely located, adequate housing or public infrastructure for growing populations (United Nations, 2014). Longstanding and new tensions such as crime, violence and disease also threaten sustainable human habitations (Barata-Salgeuiro and Erkip, 2014; King and Rathi, 2010: 7; Lanzafame and Quartesan, 2009; World Bank, 2013: 145). The increasing frequency of climate change effects such as unpredictable rainfall patterns, sea-level rise, wider and less predictable temperature extremes, and more frequent and variable extreme weather events (World Bank, 2010) also puts city-dwellers, their communities and physical environments under increased pressure. This is especially true in low- to middle-income countries (IPCC, 2014), and those with large numbers of people in poverty who often live in the most vulnerable locations and structures (UN-HABITAT, 2010). Sub-standard housing and infrastructure sometimes pose risks to social capital and social cohesion. These social resources underpin the social sustainability and resilience of the social organisation of urban communities – how people think, behave and organise themselves collectively – and the unique social strengths and capacities of individual communities: the attributes that shape their collective capacity to respond resiliently to the effects of climate change and/or natural disasters (e.g. seismic). People worldwide need to maximise their capacity to cope with, and adapt to, these pressures.

Social capital describes the networks, norms, reciprocity and trust that form the 'glue' of human communities. Social cohesion is the ability of different socio-demographic groups to live peacefully together across differences. Both concepts encompass pro-community behaviours and psychological responses as either their composite dimensions or their outcomes. These behaviours can increase communities' collective capacity, health, well-being and quality of life during routine life ('social sustainability') (Berkman, 2000; Ferlander, 2007). Simultaneously, these social resources contribute to community members' ability to cope with, adapt to, and 'bounce back' (Holling, 1996) from unplanned negative environmental events by caring for each other and their built environments in a transformative way, to ensure a healthy and sustainable continuing existence ('community resilience'). Socially planned built environments can nudge people towards adopting pro-community behaviours in routine life and during/after crises, to realise these goals.

It is well-established that the physical form and infrastructure of urban built environments and the social organisation of people are intimately connected. Built environments planned, designed, located, constructed and operated with social interaction in mind can positively influence levels of social capital and cohesion in urban networks through the relationships, social activities and cultural life that they support. Built environment structures used by millions of people – in particular housing, public areas such as squares and parks, and transport stops – are the most likely contenders for influencing pro-community behaviours, and their longer-term outcomes (referred to throughout as 'pro-community outcomes'). We focus on these three types of structures throughout. Town squares and plazas, along with public parks, sometimes located adjacent to religious or municipal institutions, have provided such spaces historically. Other non-built environment factors – such as 'individual predisposition, income, family situation, health, crime, culture' (Kelly, 2012: 9) influence levels of social interaction. However, cities provide the backdrop for the interactions of diverse masses.

When residents and users of urban areas exhibit pro-community behaviours associated with social capital and cohesion, there can be positive effects for both individuals and communities. In turn, social capital and cohesion can influence a variety of longer-term macro- and micro-level outcomes in economic development, education, job seeking, democracy, governance, health, well-being, personal security, and climate change resilience.

Whilst the potential structural and economic implications of swift urbanisation and climate science are mainstream policy discussions,[3] the social behavioural dimensions of urban social sustainability and resilience are not (Holden, 2012). These issues appear 'softer' yet harder to achieve, but they can be woven into urban planning, sustainability and resilience policies and strategies via socially aware planning. Sustainability and resilience – two high profile, buzz word concepts – are twins in efforts to prolong the resources and existence of cities for future generations, and their social components must be united in urban development research and policy. Without sustainable urban communities, there will be no human capital to create physically, economically and environmentally sustainable and resilient cities over time, by the very definition of sustainability.

Structure of the book

This study is an example of 'blue sky' conceptual thinking applied to a practical global problem. Its conceptual aim is to place the social sustainability of neighbourhood networks and their regular built environments on a continuum with their resilience to environmental adversities.

The practical aim is to identify a set of pro-community behaviours open to planner and designer application and adaptation, and recommendations for the implementation of 'socially planned built environments'. The book uses qualitative case studies to scrutinise how urban communities interact with the built environment at micro-level that quantitative approaches can overlook. It considers behaviours and psychological responses at the collective, or aggregated individual levels. The case studies offer a preliminary evidence base for those aiming to use metrics to monitor the social dimensions of urban social sustainability and resilience over time by showing dynamic development and behavioural contexts from which timely and relevant indicators may be devised.

We first review the concepts of social capital and social cohesion. We then establish urban social sustainability as a worthwhile endeavour underpinned by these concepts via: 1) policy-making, with case studies from Paraguay, Canada and Australia, and a multi-city perspective from UNESCO; and 2) the influence of neighbourhood-level urban planning, design, form and space on pro-community outcomes during periods of calm and environmental calamity. We use two pre-existing parallel theoretical frameworks devised by unconnected research teams: 1) 'sustainability of community' (Bramley and Power, 2009; Dempsey et al., 2009)[4] and 'fundamentals of neighbourhood resilience' (Zautra, Hall, and Murray, 2008) that we adapted slightly to identify the behavioural and psychological dimensions of (1) social sustainability, and (2) community resilience. We show the relationship of each dimension to social capital and social cohesion.

We applied the 'sustainability of community' frameworks to eight of the case studies across public and private sectors, and community co-led building and/or regeneration projects in India (1), the UK (3), South Africa (2), New Zealand (1), and the USA (1). They address housing, public space and transport stops. Each had explicit socially aware planning goals, and urban form and public participation influenced existing and/or potential residents' pro-community behaviours. These were, or may potentially be influenced by and during the envisioning, planning and design, and the implementation, monitoring and evaluation of the development process. Collectively, the findings point to a four-stage 'socially aware planning process'. Each case demonstrates approaches, tools and methods that urban practitioners can implement to create socially planned built environments that influence pro-community behaviours.

Six case studies from India (2), Indonesia (1), USA (1), New Zealand (1) and Bangladesh (1) were then compiled and analysed with the 'fundamentals of neighbourhood resilience' framework to demonstrate how under conditions of environmental calamity, these same and other similar behaviours enabled urban residents to cope with, and adapt to adverse impacts on their communities/built structures more or less well.

Drawing from our analyses, we offer a combined set of socially sustainable, resilient pro-community behaviours that urban development stakeholders should seek to influence. The study concludes with a preliminary action agenda of recommendations to adopt in policies, plans, programmes and projects for sustainability and resilience, emphasising processes and inclusion. This book exemplifies what social science and community development perspectives can offer, and illustrates innovative work occurring around the world. While this work is not exhaustive or representative, it provides important insights for urban development.

Notes

1 These terms are used interchangeably in the literature, see discussion in Chapter 5. We use the term 'community resilience' with our focus on neighbourhood communities. The term 'urban development' itself covers a wide range of literatures including architecture, economics, ecology, urban planning, and real estate.
2 The authors are aware of the lack of capacity for 'socially aware planning' in both the government and design professions, which demands a blend of social policy, social science and planning skills. Training and continuing education programmes as well as revisions of curricula in universities could help address these gaps.
3 The environmental, economic, physical and governance dimensions of sustainability and resilience are addressed by international organisations and programmes, various levels of government, NGOs, and academics at varying geographical scales. See, for example, United Nations Climate Summit of 2014; the Rockefeller Foundation's 100 Resilient Cities Programme, the C40 Cities Climate Leadership Group, and the World Resources Institute.
4 These papers, co-authored by the same teams, covered these dimensions between them.

References

Barata-Salgeuiro, T and Erkip, F (2014) 'Retail planning and urban resilience: an introduction to the special issue', *Cities* 36: 107–111.
Berkman, LF (2000) 'Social support, social networks, social cohesion and health', *Social Work in Health Care* 31 (2): 3–14.
Bramley, G and Power, S (2009) 'Urban form and social sustainability: the role of density and housing type', *Environment and Planning B: Planning and Design* 36: 30–48.

Dempsey, N, Bramley, G, Power, S and Brown, C (2009) 'The social dimension of sustainable development: defining urban social sustainability', *Sustainable Development* 19: 289–300.

Ferlander, S (2007) 'The importance of different forms of social capital for health', *Acta Sociologa* 50: 115–128.

Global Commission on the Economy and Climate (2014) *Better Growth, Better Climate: New Climate Economy 2014 Report*, Washington, DC: World Resources Institute, accessed on 22 December 2015 at: http://newclimateecon omy.report/wp-content/uploads/2014/08/NCE_GlobalReport.pdf

Holden, M (2012) 'Urban policy engagement with social sustainability in Metro Vancouver', *Urban Studies* 49: 527–542.

Holling, CS (1996) 'Engineering resilience versus ecological resilience', in: Schulze, P.C (ed) *Engineering Within Ecological Constraints*, Washington, DC: National Academy Press, 31–44.

IPCC (2014) Climate Change 2014: Synthesis Report. Contribution of Working Groups I, II and III to the Fifth Assessment Report of the Intergovernmental Panel on Climate Change [Core Writing Team, R.K. Pachauri and L.A. Meyer (eds)], Geneva, Switzerland, accessed 30 November 2015 at: www.ipcc.ch/report/ar5/syr/

Kelly, J-F (2012) *Social Cities*, Melbourne: Grattan Institute, accessed on 22 December 2015 at: http://grattan. edu.au/report/social-cities/

King, R and Rathi, S (2010) 'Urban Infrastructure and Climate Change in India: Constructing Environmentally Sustainable Cities', background paper prepared for *Report of High-Powered Committee on Urban Infrastructure*, Isher Ahluwalia, chair. Delhi: National Institute of Urban Affairs.

Lanzafame, F and Quartesan, A (2009) *Downtown Poverty, Methods of analysis and interventions – A sourcebook for practitioners*, Inter-American Development Bank, Washington DC, accessed on 6 December 2015 at: www.iadb.org/intal/intalcdi/PE/2009/04190a01.pdf

Oishi, S, Sherman, GD, Rothman, AJ, Snyder, M, Su, J, Zehm, K, Hertel, A.W and Hope Gonzales, M (2007) 'The socioecological model of procommunity action: the benefits of residential stability', *Journal of Personality and Social Psychology* 95(3): 831–844.

Thwaites, T (2015) 'UN Goals: Our cities hold the key to a sustainable future', *The Age*, accessed on 10 December 2015 at: www.theage.com.au/comment/un-goals-our-cities-hold-the-key-to-a-sustainable-future-20150925- gjuv13.html

United Nations (2005) *World Urbanization Prospects: The 2005 Revision*, accessed on 4 January 2016 at: www.un.org/esa/population/publications/WUP2005/2005wup.htm

United Nations Department of Economic and Social Affairs, Population Division (2014) *World Urbanization Prospects: The 2014 Revision, Highlights* (ST/ESA/SER.A/352), accessed on 26 January 2016 at: http://esa.un.org/unpd/wup/High lights/WUP2014-Highlights.pdf

United Nations Human Settlement Programme (UN-HABITAT) (2010) *State of the World's Cities 2010/2011: bridging the urban divide*, Earthscan, London, 220 pages, accessed on 27 January 2016 at: http://mirror.unhabitat.org/pmss/listItem Details.aspx?publicationID=2917

United Nations Population Fund (n.d.) accessed 26 January 2016 at: www.unfpa. org/urbanization/

World Bank (2010) *Cities and Climate Change: An Urgent Agenda.* The World Bank Urban Development Series Knowledge Papers, Volume 10. (especially Part II), Washington DC: World Bank, accessed on 6 December 2015 at: http:// siteresources.worldbank.org/INTUWM/Resources/340232-1205330656272/ CitiesandClimateChange.pdf

World Bank (2013) Brief: Social Inclusion, August 15, 2013, accessed 3 January 2016 at: www.worldbank. org/en/topic/socialdevelopment/brief/social-inclusion.

WHO (n.d.) accessed 26 January 2016 at: http://www.who.int/gho/urban_health/ situation_trends/urban_population_growth_text/en/

Zautra, A, Hall, J and Murray, K (2008) 'Community development and community resilience: an integrative approach', *Community Development* 39 (3): 130–147.

2 Spirit and methodology

The study was approached from a bottom-up anthropological perspective (without employing ethnographic methods) where we sought to examine the micro-level context of urban development. It is not, however, an anthropological study, but applies a multi-disciplinary theoretical framework to a practical urban problem, drawing from sociology, anthropology, social and environmental psychology, public policy, urban planning and design, geography, environmental studies and public health. We argue for an idealistic, broad social science starting point for the neglected behavioural side of sustainability and resilience. The book should be read for its new ideas, how things should be rather than necessarily how they are right now, within the limits of formal planning regimes. It may be categorised as a form of applied (practical) social science and urban policy research.

We acknowledge the highly political nature of development and the power disparities and inequities between its stakeholders: city authorities, landowners, private and public sector builders, NGOs, communities and individuals. Like others, we recognise them collectively as urban change agents (Beard *et al.*, 2016). We recognise the limits of the public's power to be involved and influence development in their interests, especially in low- to middle-income countries. Within these limits, we also champion the importance of creative organic, often informal, development, and more formal community-led or co-led developments. Additionally, this book underemphasises the broader policy environment that is of utmost importance but is not our focus here.[1] However, while we promote the actions that people can take for themselves, our priority here is persuading all development stakeholders from all sectors to consider social issues through the evidence presented. Thus some cases are more top-heavy or developer-led or controlled than others. However, our recommendations emphasise inclusion and processes, building on insights from our cases.

We began by establishing that the 'social sustainability' concept has been adopted by supra-national organisations (Stren and Polese, 2000;

Woodcraft, 2012) in regional and city policy frameworks (Berkeley Group, 2014; Woodcraft, 2012), and within the planning and construction sector at neighbourhood level (Berkeley Group, 2014; Woodcraft, 2012) with the concept more frequently applied to urban development in higher-income countries (Woodcraft, 2012). We reviewed the literature on social capital and social cohesion, social sustainability and social/community resilience to construct our theoretical framework. We then collated case-study materials. We examined innovative plans and projects from any country that enabled us to collate significant projected and actual[2] built environment-influenced pro-community behaviours to demonstrate their global significance, and cases that show the link between built environments and social behaviour under environmental duress.

Case-study content was taken from secondary academic studies and organisations' project documentation as located through reviews, approaching organisations, and internet research conducted by interns.[3] Selection criteria for the only few available sources containing behavioural information were descriptive data demonstrating the intricate and dynamic interactions and relationships between built environments, human behaviour and/or environmental crises, and creative ideas for recommendations. While all studies contain qualitative data, four social sustainability cases[4] (but no resilience cases) included some behavioural metrics. However, we prioritised identifying, *not* quantifying, the exhibition of behaviours, and ideas for socially aware planning. Additionally, most sources did not include much background detail on city development and regulatory perspectives. We had no involvement in any cases.

We sought 'social sustainability' case studies covering every continent and the global north/south. In practice, there were few documented examples from the south although the issues are pertinent with most rapid urbanisation expected in low- and middle-income countries, and far more 'resilience' examples of the interaction of the built environment and communities experiencing disasters from this region. This imbalance reflects where the majority of climate changed-related impacts fall (IPCC, 2014; Karuppannan and Sivam, 2011), and the nature of the scholarship in different areas, highlighting the need for a bi-directional exchange of practical ideas between north/south as well as across different academic communities.

We analysed the sources using our own questions:

(a) Does this case illustrate an example of social sustainability, community resilience or both?
(b) Is it a major case study or a passing example to illustrate a point?

(c)   In this case, how does the urban planning process or design of the built environment impact on dimensions of social capital, social cohesion and pro-community behaviours?

(d)   What behavioural and psychological insights does this case provide?

(e)   What key points does it raise about the planning and design process?

(f)   What are the lessons of the case?

(g)   What does it tell us about why this story is important now – the global circumstances that merit its inclusion in this study?

(h)   What makes this story so compelling – why is it different from other possibilities?

We also analysed them using the two pre-existing and published frameworks by unconnected research teams: 1) 'sustainability of community': based on a literature review on urban social sustainability that defined theoretical dimensions that urban form could influence;[5] and 2) 'fundamentals of neighbourhood resilience': which reviewed 22 health and community development studies to generate theoretical dimensions of 'resilient processes'. We used the findings of our literature review of social capital and social cohesion to determine how each dimension was related to these concepts – as a sub-component or outcome.

All dimensions were grounded in the actions and/or psychological states of people living in neighbourhoods, or social processes encompassing both, apart from the physical 'formal and informal places for civic gathering' dimension in framework 2.[6] We emphasised the behavioural/psychological division as social capital theory divides the concept into structural (behavioural formations: networks) and cognitive (norms, trust) forms that may/may not interact to produce further outcomes, e.g. sense of belonging. Likewise, referencing dimensions from framework 1, an affective concept[7] such as 'pride in and attachment to the neighbourhood' may/may not motivate a person to 'participate in collective or civic activities'.[8] Development should promote states of mind that lead to positive action, and behaviours that produce a pro-community state of mind may lead to great proactivity. We observed which theoretical dimensions applied in real projects, new ones that occurred in the case studies as influenced by the built environment/development, and all those that overlapped between the sustainability and resilience cases.

We reconstructed the central built environment/behavioural narratives in our own words for every case. We contacted and obtained case-study feedback from all but three organisations out of the original authors[9] through non-response or missing contact details. The policy recommendations were created through analysis of the 'lessons' identified from cases using our experience in urban development research and practice. There were several methodological challenges in producing this book. While we recognise the dynamic nature of the featured 'communities', many of the data sources did not provide broad contextual data on their inner workings as they were written from an urban development perspective rather than a social science one. The complex interaction of behavioural factors with non-behavioural factors such as economics, poverty, power, social and spatial inequities, and other social groups within the same cities were mostly not highlighted in the source materials. As a result, our case studies may appear simplistic, but they meet our clear intention of highlighting the interactions between built structures, social organisation and associated pro-community behaviours, and environmental adversities. We recognise these as limitations in the context of the few available studies that address urban development, behavioural and psychological responses together. Indeed, we view this book as an attempt to begin to forge a dialogue among these fields.

Figure 2.1 Portland neighbourhood squares
Source: Jan Semenza

Notes

1 See for example, UN HABITAT (2016) for an excellent review of these issues at a global level.
2 Two of the 'social sustainability' case studies: 1) Belfast housing and 2) Christchurch's Bus Xchange, were unrealised plans due to 1) financial turmoil and 2) earthquakes. Both plans drew upon extensive social research with potential tenant and user communities. These data were used to predict behavioural responses using CB's experience in working on *ex-ante* social and health impact assessments (HIA and SIA). The social data elicited from both involved communities included strong ideas for socially aware planning, also put forward by the anthropologists conducting social research with communities in the Belfast neighbourhoods around the planned housing complex.
3 See Acknowledgements page.
4 Portland, Manchester, southern England, Delhi.
5 This review covered the British context, and our research tested how these dimensions were applicable in other contexts.
6 We limited ourselves to applying the dimensions in these frameworks, and not other possible dimensions. This is because the social sustainability dimensions were strictly linked to the influence of the built environment, and the resilience dimensions were located within the neighbourhood, the spatial context of our study.
7 Psychological functioning comprises different mechanisms: e.g. cognitive, affective, behavioural, deliberative. See, for example, Ferrer and Klein (2015), Lench *et al.* (2013).
8 The many ways in which the 'sustainability of community' dimensions can influence each other are covered in Dempsey et al. (2009).
9 Cases from Cape Town (2), and Surat (2), were checked by other experts.

References

Beard, VA, Mahendra, A and Westphal, MI (2016) 'Towards a More Equitable City: Framing the Challenges and Opportunities.' Working Paper. World Resources Report. Washington, DC: World Resources Institute.

Berkeley Group (2014) *Creating Successful Places: A Toolkit*, accessed on 6 December 2015 at: www. berkeleygroup.co.uk/media/pdf/l/h/berkeley-social-sustainability-toolkit.pdf.

Dempsey, N, Bramley, G, Power, S and Brown, C (2009) 'The social dimension of sustainable development: defining urban social sustainability', *Sustainable Development* 19: 289–300.

Ferrer, RA and Klein, WMP (2015) 'Risk perceptions and health behaviour', *Current Opinion in Psychology* 5: 85–89.

IPCC (2014) *Climate Change 2014: Synthesis Report. Contribution of Working Groups I, II and III to the Fifth Assessment Report of the Intergovernmental Panel on Climate Change* [Core Writing Team, R.K. Pachauri and L.A. Meyer (eds)], Geneva, Switzerland, accessed 30 November 2015 at: www.ipcc.ch/report/ar5/syr/.

Karuppannan, S and Sivam, A (2011) 'Social sustainability and neighbourhood design: an investigation of residents' satisfaction in Delhi', *Local Environment: The International Journal of Justice and Sustainability* 16 (9): 849–870.

Lench, HC, Darbor, KE and Berg, LA (2013) 'Functional perspectives on emotion, behavior, and cognition', *Behavioral Sciences* 3 (4): 536–540.

Stren, R and Polese, M (2000) *The Social Sustainability of Cities: Diversity and the Management of Change*, Toronto: University of Toronto Press.

Woodcraft, S (2012) 'Social sustainability and new communities: moving from concept to practice in the UK', *Procedia – Social and Behavioural Sciences* 68: 29–42.

3 Social sustainability in routine daily life

What is social sustainability?

Current global pressures mean that urban policymakers and practitioners must learn how to incorporate the social dimension of sustainable development – social sustainability – into projects, policies and strategies, so that city residents may withstand such pressures. These development stakeholders need to understand what social sustainability is, how it relates to the planning, placement, design, construction and operation of city places, and ultimately, to human behaviour. We start with this first question: what is social sustainability?

Social sustainability is an ideal that can be defined as the: 'viability, health and functioning of "society" itself as a collective entity' (Dempsey *et al.*, 2009: 290), or at local level, a 'community'. Its 'viability, health and functioning' depends on how people relate to, and behave towards each other, communicate, and collectively organise themselves. Societies can exist at national or local level, with national societies being the largest scale at which people organise the way they live together. Societies contain many institutions and systems where people interact and conduct relationships that help them to meet their needs. These include state agencies and institutions, places of employment, education, civic and civil institutions and organisations, religions and cultures.

Within a national society and on a smaller scale of human organisation, regions, cities and neighbourhoods contain populations. This book is focused on the local face-to-face scale of social interaction, primarily within neighbourhoods, and the networks or communities who live there.[1] Some communities are defined by spatial proximity – such as within the city, neighbourhood or street – and relationships between local residents. Others come about through shared characteristics, e.g. ethnicity, kinship, religion and culture, or interests, e.g. politics or employment, or circumstances, e.g. shared experience of a disaster (McAslan, 2010: 6). People may identify with and consider they belong to many communities, or indeed none.

The Western sociological origins of 'community' have been highly influential in traditional understandings of the socio-residential community (Tönnies, 1887): where local residence is synonymous with belonging to a social network or supportive social group. In practice, local networks may be strong or weak (Coutts *et al.*, 2007), and may or may not emerge as social communities, with shared goals/purpose as well as common interests. Moreover, communities themselves can be inherently hierarchical, with self-nominated leaders having inadequate transparency and accountability, and power unevenly distributed between leaders and members. Network or community members or leaders may not always act for the 'common good'. Communities are dynamic, and their character and composition are subject to change. In some societies, neighbourhood networks may be thought of in another way, and under another name. But to the extent that city residents share some common experience of the daily life in their neighbourhood, they may identify with the idea of a social community or in the very least, a local network. It is difficult to separate social activity from its physical location (Blackman, 2006).

Members of local networks may be family or neighbours living in close proximity, members of a religious community or other social grouping. The important point for our argument is that they are located nearby and offer network membership: the building block of social capital. Historic social theories of communities (Baldwin, 2012) linked them with collective identities, whilst urban planning discourses have taken it for granted that neighbourhoods have place-based identities that somehow represent both their characteristics and actual residents. Neighbourhoods are places where people live, and the areas around a specific space, yet the term is also used to refer to the neighbourly feeling of the place, providing that place-based identity (Mumford, 1954). In modern times some communities are not dependent on geographic location, such as online communities or nostalgic 'communities-in-the-mind' (Pahl, 2005: 633) where social life can be anonymous and dispersed: people interact in different networks – 'personal communities' (Pahl, 2005; Morgan, 2005) that are not necessarily centred on the socio-residential community (Baldwin, 2012). However, the source of resilience to the impacts of climate change and environmental shocks lies deep within place-based, local networks, and people's everyday behaviours and psychological responses. Resilience requires benevolent social activities driven by 'positive' pro-community behaviours among locally proximate people within these co-reacting, overlapping spatial and social entities of neighbourhood and community. It is these aspects that we would like to see supported to enable city-dwellers to cope and adapt. Power and resource distributions, leaders and social dynamics fluctuate and change, but the built environment can contribute to a total enabling environment for the development of social capital, cohesion and pro-community behaviours.

Social sustainability in policy and research

This section considers how researchers and policymakers have thought about social sustainability. In policy and research on social sustainability, a question arises: which aspects of social organisation should be sustained? For whom? And who makes that choice? Policymakers and academics have failed to arrive at a single answer or definition of social sustainability (Dempsey *et al.*, 2009: 290; Woodcraft, 2012: 30). A broad view holds that 'economic, social and cultural conditions, efforts and values are deemed to be resources that also need to be preserved for future generations' (Littig and Greissler, 2005: 67).

In international development, major institutions have identified some of these resources. The UK's Department for International Development (DfID) prioritised social equity and minimising social exclusion (DfID, 1999: 1.4), whilst finding that social sustainability 'should incorporate normative implications of sustainability such as gender equity, social justice and quality of life' (Konig, 2002: 69). At the World Bank, social sustainability was thought to comprise 'equity, social mobility, social cohesion, participation, empowerment, cultural identity and institutional development' (Serageldin, 1996: 3). In developed regions, the idea of social sustainability has largely been operationalised through national social welfare policies (Murphy, 2012: 26), social policy and community development (for example: Europe – Konig, 2002; Canada – Cooper, 2006 and Holden, 2012; Australia – McKenzie, 2004; Northern hemisphere – Murphy, 2012: 16). We address social sustainability in the context of urban development in Chapter 4.

Our literature review of policy and research in global academia revealed that ideas of social sustainability – aside from the aspects related to urban form – contain the following common items, shown in Table 3.1.

Other work has identified common themes across the many academic interpretations of social sustainability: 'philosophical and political ideas of human rights, well-being, equality and social justice, to related ideas of community social capital and empowerment' (Woodcraft *et al.*, 2011:

Table 3.1 Common items making up 'social sustainability'

Item	Author/s
Meeting of basic and non-basic needs for quality of life	McKenzie (2004: 12); Littig and Griessler (2005: 71); Konig (2002: 70); Bramley *et al.* (2009); Bramley and Power (2009); Woodcraft (2012: 35)
Equity, equality and inclusion-related measures to facilitate social and economic justice	McKenzie (2004: 23); Konig (2002: 70); Karuppannan and Sivam (2011: 851); Dempsey *et al.* (2009); Murphy (2012: 19)
Opportunities for participation in democracy – especially community governance	McKenzie (2004: 13); Karuppannan and Sivam (2011: 851); Dempsey *et al.* (2009: 295); Woodcraft (2012: 35); Murphy (2012: 19)
Social capital, social integration and social cohesion	Konig, (2002); Bramley *et al.* (2009); Bramley and Power (2009); Dempsey *et al.* (2009: 293–295); Polese and Stren (2000: 15–16); McKenzie (2004: 12); Karuppannan and Sivam (2011: 851); Murphy (2012: 19)
Identity and attachments to place and community	Bramley *et al.* (2009); Bramley and Power (2009); Dempsey *et al.* (2011)
Happiness and well-being	Littig and Griessler (2005); Colantonio (2008: 8)
Conditions that preserve social sustainability for future generations	Chambers and Conway (1992: 14–17), discussed in Konig (2002: 69); McKenzie (2004: 12); Dubois (2005: 7)

31). The term is ambiguous and contested, and will remain so as a result of its political nature.

However, in both policy and research, there is a general consensus around three concepts that underpin it: social capital, human capital, and well-being (Colantonio and Dixon, 2010; Dempsey *et al.*, 2009; Murphy, 2012; Magee *et al.*, 2012, quoted in Woodcraft, 2012: 31; Weingaertner and Moberg, 2011). Social capital is central to our argument, whilst human capital is an important resource for ensuring that cities are sustainable and resilient. Well-being is a pro-community outcome that socially sustainable urban communities should be able to achieve.

Whatever social resources societies and communities have to contribute to their 'viability, health and functioning', social sustainability is not a static social condition, an end goal that can be met and abandoned. Rather social sustainability is a dynamic ideal, and a process (Dempsey *et al.*, 2009: 292; McKenzie, 2004: 22; Sachs, 1999: 32–33) surrounding the fluctuating strength and effectiveness of its constituent resources. People can work towards strengthening these resources. When these are said to be strong and effective, a society or community may be more socially sustainable. The social resources that should be sustained in each nation, society or community are dependent on context (including political priorities), social values and culture (Karuppannan and Sivam, 2011: 850).

Social capital

This section reviews the concept of social capital. The level of positive social capital and social cohesion in a neighbourhood can influence the effectiveness of local structures of social organisation, and the strength of a network or community's social resources (Forrest and Kearns, 2001: 2130 and 2137). Social capital is a social science concept that is contested, variously defined and dynamic. It explains the benefits that people can accrue when interacting and working together in social networks (based on the work of Bourdieu, 1985; Coleman, 1988a,b; Portes, 1998; Putnam, 1993, 2000). Networks are formed when people share common cognitive attributes, such as norms and trust that help them organise and prioritise their relationships with others.

Social capital breaks down into two forms: cognitive (mental) and structural (Coutts *et al.*, 2007: 5; Grootaert and van Bastelaer, 2001: 5). The cognitive form describes 'the mental processes and perceptions' (Sherrieb *et al.*, 2010: 243) derived from cognitive attributes: behavioural norms, expectation of reciprocal acts, trust, values, attitudes, and beliefs that people share with others – family members, friends, neighbours and colleagues – that influence cooperative behaviours such as forming networks. Behavioural norms tell people how to behave in acceptable ways in networks in which they interact, so that they maintain trust with others, and can expect mutual reciprocal acts of help and support. The structural form of social capital is the networks themselves, such as informal neighbourhood networks or the semi-formal networks at civic associations (Putnam, 1993, 2000). Social structures – which can include dense networks, patterns of civic engagement, and established roles (Coutts *et al.*, 2007: 6; Grootaert and van Bastelaer, 2001: 5) – are the scaffolding for our social relationships. Networks come about through social (or virtual) interaction and connections leading to repeated participation in a networked group of people, therefore networks evolve from behavioural acts.

The cognitive form of social capital does not make much sense without the structural form. Behavioural norms and trust are also shaped by factors such as 'personal characteristics, institutional or geographic contexts' (Coutts *et al.*, 2007: 14). The basic idea of social capital is that its two forms work together, and are complementary, but it is not guaranteed. Strong cognitive bonds may exist outside a 'formal structural arrangement' – for example, participating in a civic association may not mean that members develop such bonds, especially if membership is not voluntary (Grootaert and van Bastelaer, 2001: 6).

The cognitive/structural distinction is important to bear in mind when separating out key aspects of how social capital works, e.g. 1) the place or situation where it occurs, such as a neighbourhood; 2) the people participating in networks; 3) their shared norms or trust that facilitate group interactions and collaborations; and 4) the advantages they hope to or can gain from participation (and hence any party providing these benefits (Portes, 1998: 6)). Social capital is treated in this book as an outcome of group activity rather than a property of individuals, although it can be both (Ferlander, 2007: 117). However, people and households create social capital as members of networks (Woolcock and Narayan, 2000: 231).

Known negative effects and outcomes of social capital and cohesion include the control and constraints exercised through the expectation of mutual obligations in tight-knit networks, e.g. the mafia (Forrest and Kearns, 2001: 2141; Portes, 1998: 15; Woolcock and Narayan, 2000: 231). However, we focus on the positive aspects that can be harnessed to benefit communities under stress. In policy, social capital is usually treated as something to develop for the 'good' of a community. For a neighbourhood group of residents collaborating on an urban project, the benefits or outcomes will span a wide range. Table 3.2 shows example benefits for urban development, and their uses.

Social capital has been linked to positive macro and micro-level outcomes: economic growth and development (Grootaert and van Bastelaer, 2001: iii; Portes, 1998: 19), democracy (Putnam, 1993), better quality governance (Putnam, 1993, 2000), less crime (OECD, 2001: 54; Portes, 1998: 19), health (OECD, 2001: 52; Putnam, 2000: 326), subjective well-being or life satisfaction (Helliwell and Putnam, 2004: 1444; OECD, 2001: 55), educational achievement (Coleman, 1988a), finding jobs (Barbieri, Russell and Paugam, 1999), child welfare (Putnam, 2000), and coping with climate change (Adger, 2003).

There are several distinct forms of social capital. *Bonding social capital* is the formation of strong bonds between members of groups

Table 3.2 Benefits and outcomes of social capital, and their uses in urban development

Benefit/outcome	Example uses for benefit
Information sharing, and collective action and decision making	Collective benefit – poor communities can tackle poverty, resolve disputes, source new opportunities
Cash loans, labour in kind, completion of a building project	Urban infrastructure and development that the community have a stake in
Better relations among diverse residents of a neighbourhood (social cohesion)	Improved feelings of safety, stronger collective ability to work together
Attachments or personal identification to/with a place or community	Psychosocial attachments motivate positive pro-community behaviours
Norms of reciprocity leading to emotional support	Emotional support leads to better health and well-being
Enhanced feelings of safety	Improves social cohesion
Enhanced feelings of empowerment	Improves public participation in civic activities

who share common characteristics, such as family members, neighbours, close friends and colleagues. Bonds help people to negotiate norms that dictate acceptable social behaviours, elicit mutual help, and protect vulnerable individuals (Coutts *et al.*, 2007: 1). *Bridging social capital* occurs between groups who differ strongly from each other – by socio-demographic characteristics such as socio-economic status, ethnicity and occupation. It creates weak ties between people based on formal or informal social interaction (Coutts *et al.*, 2007: 1–2).

Poorer people, for example, may have intense *bonding social capital* based on shared experience. They may, however, lack the *bridging social capital* needed to make external connections that help them to leverage upwards, and escape poverty or improve neighbourhood conditions through collective action (Woolcock and Narayan, 2000: 227). *Horizontal social capital* refers to connections between people and groups of equal or near equal status in a hierarchy. *Vertical (linking) social capital* links groups of people to other groups or institutions with more power, resources or status (Coutts *et al.*, 2007: 6).

Social cohesion

Social cohesion is a broader academic and policy concept closely related to social capital. It describes the extent to which people from the same community or society get along, trust each other, and live peacefully

together with or without social, ethnic and other demographic dif
(for example, see Cantle, 2001; Council of Europe, 2004; OECD, 200
lack of cohesion may result in more tense and conflictual interactions. Soci
cohesion at neighbourhood level is underpinned by some factors or pre-
conditions that promote harmonious behaviour, whereas a lack of cohesion
is exacerbated by preconditions resulting in more conflictual behaviour
among people living in physical proximity to each other. Causal factors are
both social and economic. Table 3.3 describes the factors contributing to
social cohesion, and how their absence may hinder cohesion.

Table 3.3 Factors underpinning social cohesion

Social factors needed for social cohesion	What a lack of cohesion would look like without these social factors	Economic factors needed for social cohesion	What a lack of cohesion would look like without these economic factors
Shared morality and common purpose – common values and a civic culture (including participation in democracy and legal rights)	Disparate moral values, lack of civic and political participation and collaboration	Meeting of basic needs, including welfare needs through sufficient economic activity and/or social safety net (Council of Europe, 2004: 5)	Human beings unable to function
Social control and social order (as transmitted through behavioural norms whilst interacting in networks)	Social disorder and conflict	Perceived fairness in access to economic opportunity	Social/political disorder resulting from many feeling the system is unfair
Level of social interaction within families and communities (social capital)	Low levels of social interaction between and within communities	Socio-economic equity and inclusion.	Extreme socio-economic inequality
Place and community attachment and identity (formed through interacting in networks)	Low levels of place and community attachment		

Source: Adapted from Forrest and Kearns (2001: 2128–2129).

Figure 3.1 Manchester participatory urban design intervention
Source: Jamie Anderson.

Local relationships may be socially cohesive if underpinned by some of these factors. For example, when people act according to the accepted norms of the neighbourhood, share an attachment to and identify with the community and neighbourhood, they may develop bonds with other residents. We recognise that norms may be constraining for some and a source of conformity that people may seek to escape. Norms are also dynamic and can change. However, what we are describing here is an ideal-type theory that provides a basis for understanding cohesion. Conversely, when there are greater income disparities between neighbours, these may create a basis for tension and conflict. At policy level, people are more likely to feel responsibility for, and be willing to contribute to their community and society (Ferroni, Mateo and Payne, 2008: 4) when their basic needs for work, welfare and so on are met.

Social cohesion occurs when the quality of interactions and communications in family and community networks in a place, as influenced by these pre-conditions, is high (Kearns and Forrest, 2000: 999). Cohesion is therefore a possible outcome (and source) of a community having social capital (Berger-Schmitt, 2000; Ferlander, 2007: 115; Ferroni, Mateo and Payne, 2008: 4) (e.g. strong networks/positive interactions) and social capital can be 'the practical tool to achieve social cohesion' (Zetter *et al.*, 2006: 22) (e.g. harmonious relationships). A strong indicator of high levels of social cohesion in a neighbourhood is said to be the extent to which a wide array of people will get together to promote or defend a community interest (Forrest and Kearns, 2001: 2124). Such community participation can subsequently contribute to positive well-being, thereby cohesion may indirectly influence well-being (Forrest and Kearns, 2001: 2130). As with the ideal of social sustainability, a network of socially cohesive residents is not a goal that can be achieved and discarded (Jenson, 2010: 7) or a characteristic of individuals, but an ideal situation that must constantly be striven for (Jenson, 2010: 15).

Our definition of social cohesion is thus: social cohesion happens when people from the same community or society get along, trust each other, and live peacefully together with or without social or ethnic differences. This is supported by economic equality and inclusion, democracy, basic needs being met, and social solidarity between people. Our emphasis is on social cohesion at local neighbourhood level (Forrest and Kearns, 2001). However, it has been discussed and addressed at international level in research and policy; for example, in the EU's Treaty of Maastricht in 1992 and Lisbon Agenda of 1995 (Jensen, 2010); in various OECD documents (e.g. OECD, 1997, 2006); and by the United Nations Economic Commission for Latin America and the Caribbean (ECLAC), discussed in Tokman (2007), Council of Europe (2004); World Bank and Inter-American Development Bank in Ferroni, Mateo and Payne (2008); and national level, especially through national policy frameworks, for example, in France, Canada, New Zealand, Denmark, Australia, see Ferroni, Mateo and Payne (2008) and Jenson (2010).

Social capital and cohesion, their component parts and outcomes should be regarded as social resources of neighbourhood networks that can be invested in to strengthen people's capacity to tackle problems collectively. Below we offer a case study from the village of Santa Ana in Paraguay: a community with ample social capital and cohesion, who have successfully collectively maintained their infrastructure. It suggests that good relations can motivate people to care for and take care of the place where they live. Social science concepts from our analysis are shown in square brackets in the text.

Social capital and social cohesion in Santa Ana, Paraguay

Residents of the village of Santa Ana, Paraguay, are a homogenous group [*population characteristic*] with a strong sense of civic duty [*cognitive social capital*] and trusted local leaders [*cognitive* (trust) and *structural* (leadership role) *social capital*]. These factors combined have resulted in strong overall social capital, which contributes to exceptional social cohesion, and have enabled the community to take responsibility for the collective maintenance of its infrastructure. Although the government constructed roads, electricity lines and water supply, residents contribute by maintaining these, along with bridges, when repairs are required. (World Bank, 2014: 148).

Horizontal social capital among the population, and vertical social capital between the population, its leadership and the government – for providing infrastructure and allowing collective maintenance – are both present here. The social relationships in the village and initially poor infrastructure may have motivated the civic sense of duty. The key active behaviours and cognitive components on display are: a) belief in the common good (*cognitive*), b) trust in leadership (*cognitive*) and c) collective action – participation in maintenance of infrastructure (*active behaviour*).

Although not representative of most communities due to its homogeneity, this unusual case from Latin America shows how social capital and cohesion contribute to positive outcomes when behavioural and cognitive components are connected to a community's infrastructure. Within formal strategies, city governments and planners can support communities to have some control over their infrastructure in ways that both harness and reinforce social capital and cohesion, preferably when collective maintenance provides meaningful opportunities for self-employment for individuals.

Note

1 We acknowledge that the physical, economic and social environments of spatially and administratively defined neighbourhoods are shaped and negotiated in terms of their relationship to the wider city and its administration. However, we are focused on local-scale social interaction.

References

Adger, WN (2003) 'Social capital, collective action, and adaptation to climate change', *Economic Geography* 79: (4): 387–404.

Baldwin, C (2012) *Locating Britishness? Mediating identity, ethnicity, community and place in multi-ethnic Swindon*. Unpublished DPhil thesis. Oxford: University of Oxford.

Barbieri, P, Russell, H and Paugam, S (1999) 'Social capital and exits from unemployment', unpublished paper, OECD.

Berger-Schmitt, R (2000) *Social Cohesion as an Aspect of the Quality of Societies: Concept and Measurement*, Center for Survey Research and Methodology (ZUMA), EU Report Working Paper no 14, Mannheim, Germany.

Blackman, T (2006) *Placing Health: Neighbourhood Renewal, Health Improvement and Complexity.* Bristol, UK: Policy.

Bourdieu, P (1985) 'The forms of capital', in: Richardson, JG (ed.) *Handbook for Theory and Research for the Sociology of Education*, New York: Greenwood, 241–258.

Bramley, G and Power, S (2009) 'Urban form and social sustainability: the role of density and housing type', *Environment and Planning B: Planning and Design* 36: 30–48.

Bramley, G, Dempsey, N, Power, S, Brown, C and Watkins, D (2009) 'Social sustainability and urban form: evidence from Five British cities', *Environment and Planning A* 41: 2125–2142.

Cantle, T (2001) *Community Cohesion: A Report of the Independent Review Team*, London: Home Office.

Chambers, R and Conway, G (1992) *Sustainable Rural Livelihoods: Practical Concepts for the 21st Century.* Sussex Discussion Paper 296. Brighton, UK: Institute of Development Studies.

Colantonio, A (2008) *Traditional and Emerging Prospects in Social Sustainability in Measuring Social Sustainability: Best Practice from Urban Renewal in the EU* 2008/02: EIBURS Working Paper Series November 2008, 1-27, accessed on 23 December 2015 at: http://oisd.brookes.ac.uk/sustainable_communities/resources/SocialSustainabilityProspectspaper.pdf

Colantonio, A and Dixon, T (2010) *Urban Regeneration and Social Sustainability: Best Practice from European Cities*, Oxford: John Wiley & Sons.

Coleman, JS (1988a) 'Social capital in the creation of human capital', *American Journal of Sociology* 94: S95–121.

Coleman, JS (1988b) 'The creation and destruction of social capital: implications for the law', *Notre Dame Journal of Law, Ethics, Public Policy* 3: 375–404.

Cooper, M (2006) *Social Sustainability in Vancouver.* Research Report F62. Ottawa: Family Network. Canadian Policy Research Networks, accessed on 23 December 2015 at: http://rcrpp.org/documents/45693_en.pdf

Council of Europe/European Commission for Social Cohesion (CDCS) (2004) *Revised Strategy for Social Cohesion.* Strasbourg: CDCS.

Coutts, A, Ramos Pinto, P, Cave, B, and Kawachi, I (2007) *Social Capital Indicators in the UK: A research project for the Commission for Racial Equality*, Leeds and London: Ben Cave Associates and Commission for Racial Equality.

DFID (1999) *Sustainable Livelihoods Guidance Sheets. Department for International Development*, Government of the United Kingdom, accessed during 2014 at:www.efls.ca/webresources/DFID_Sustainable_livelihoods_guidance_sheet.pdf

Dempsey, N, Bramley, G, Power, S and Brown, C (2009) 'The social dimension of sustainable development: defining urban social sustainability', *Sustainable Development* 19: 289–300.

Dubois, J-L (2005) 'The Search for Socially Sustainable Development: Conceptual and methodological issues', Paper presented at the International Conference in

Kyoto: Ethics, Economics and Law against injustice, Ristumeikan University, October 28–30, 2005.

Ferlander, S (2007) 'The importance of different forms of social capital for health', *Acta Sociologa* 50: 115–128.

Ferroni, M, Mateo, M and Payne, M (2008) *Development under Conditions of Inequality and Trust: Social Cohesion in Latin America*, IFPRI Discussion Paper 00777, Washington DC: International Food Policy Research Institute.

Forrest, R and Kearns, A (2001) 'Social cohesion, social capital and the neighbourhood', *Urban Studies* 38 (12): 2125–2143.

Grootaert, C and van Bastelaer, T (2001) *Understanding and Measuring Social Capital: A Synthesis of Findings and Recommendations from the Social Capital Initiative*, Social Capital Initiative Working paper No. 24., The World Bank Social Development Family. Washington DC: World Bank, accessed on 22 December 2015 at: http://siteresources.worldbank.org/INTSOCIALCAPITAL/Resources/Social-Capital-Initiative-Working-Paper-Series/SCI-WPS-24.pdf

Helliwell, JF and Putnam, RD (2004) 'The social context of well-being', *Philosophical Transactions of the Royal Society B: Biological Sciences* 359 (1449): 1435–1446.

Holden, M (2012) 'Urban policy engagement with social sustainability in metro Vancouver', *Urban Studies* 49: 527–542.

Jenson, J (2010) *Defining and Measuring Social Cohesion*. London: Commonwealth Secretariat and United Nations Research Institute for Sustainable Development, accessed on 23 December 2015 at: www.unrisd.org/80256B3C005BCCF9ch/170C271B7168CC30C12577D0004BA206?OpenDocument.

Karuppannan, S and Sivam, A (2011) 'Social sustainability and neighbourhood design: an investigation of residents' satisfaction in Delhi', *Local Environment: The International Journal of Justice and Sustainability* 16 (9): 849–870.

Kearns, A and Forrest, R (2000) 'Social cohesion and multilevel urban Governance', *Urban Studies* 37: 995–1017.

Konig, J (2002) *Social sustainability in a globalizing world: context, theory and methodology explored*, The Hague: UNESCO, accessed on 22 December 2015 at: http://portal.unesco.org/shs/fr/files/7596/11120888871moreonmost.pdf/moreonmost.pdf#page=61

Littig, B and Greissler, E (2005) 'Social sustainability: a catchword between political pragmatism and social theory', *International Journal of Sustainable Development* 8 (12): 65–79.

McAslan, A (2010) *Community Resilience: Understanding the Concept and its Application*. Australia: Torrens Resilience Institute, accessed on 22 December 2015 at: http://sustainablecommunitiessa.files.wordpress.com/2011/06/community-resilience-from-torrens-institute.pdf

McKenzie, S (2004) *Social Sustainability: Towards some Definitions*. Magill, South Australia: Hawke Research Institute, University of South Australia, 1–29.

Magee, L, Scerri, A and James, P (2012) 'Measuring social sustainability: a community-centred approach', *Applied Research in Quality of Life* 7(3): 239–

261. Accessed on 22 December 2015 at: www.springerlink.com.libproxy.ucl.ac. uk/content/6887603286343817/abstract/

Morgan, DHJ (2005) 'Revisiting "Communities in Britain"', *The Sociological Review* 53 (4): 641–657.

Mumford, L (1954) 'The neighborhood and the neighborhood unit,' *The Town Planning Review* 24 (4): 256–270.

Murphy, K (2012) 'The social pillar of sustainable development: a literature review and framework for policy analysis', *Sustainability: Science, Practice and Policy* 8 (1): 15–29.

Pahl, R (2005) 'Are all communities communities in the mind?' *The Sociological Review* 53 (4): 621–640.

OECD. (1997) *Beyond 2000: The New Social Policy Agenda*. Paris: OECD.

OECD. (2001) *The Well-being of Nations: The Role of Human and Social Capital*. Paris: OECD.

OECD. (2006) *Competitive Cities in the Global Economy*, OECD Territorial Reviews. Paris: OECD.

Polese, M and Stren, R (2000) *The Social Sustainability of Cities: Diversity and the Management of Change*. Toronto: University of Toronto Press.

Portes, A (1998) 'Social Capital: its origins and applications in modern sociology', *Annual Review of Sociology* 24 (1): 24.

Putnam, R (1993) *Making Democracy Work: Civic Traditions in Modern Italy*, Princeton, NJ: Princeton University Press.

Putnam, RD (2000) *Bowling Alone: The Collapse and Revival of American Community*, New York: Simon & Schuster.

Sachs, I (1999) 'Social sustainability and whole development: exploring the dimensions of sustainable development', Becker, E and Jahn, T (eds) *Sustainability and the Social Sciences: A Cross-disciplinary Approach to Integrating Environmental Considerations into Theoretical Reorientation*, London: ZED Books.

Serageldin, I (1996) *Sustainability and the Wealth of Nations: First Steps in an Ongoing Journey*. Environmentally sustainable development studies and monographs series; no. 5*ESSD Environmentally & Socially Sustainable Development Work in Progress. Washington, D.C: The World Bank, accessed on 22 December 2015 at: http://documents.worldbank.org/curated/en/1996/07/696375/ sustainability-wealth-nations-first-steps-ongoing-journey

Sherrieb, K, Norris, FH and Galea, S (2010) 'Measuring capacities for community resilience', *Social Indicators Research* 99: 227–247.

Tokman, VE (2007) 'The informal economy, insecurity, and social cohesion in Latin America', *International Labour Review*, 146 (1–2): 81–107.

Tönnies, F (1887) *Community and Society*, New York: Harper Torchbooks.

Weingaertner, C and Moberg, A (2011) 'Exploring social sustainability: learning from perspectives on urban development and companies and products', *Sustainable Development* 22 (2): 122–133.

Woodcraft, S (2012) 'Social sustainability and new communities: moving from concept to practice in the UK', *Procedia – Social and Behavioural Sciences* 68: 29–42.

Woodcraft, S, Bacon, N, Caistor-Arendar, L and Hackett, T, with Sir Peter Hall (2011) *Design for Social Sustainability: A Framework for Creating Thriving New Communities*. London: Social Life, accessed on 23 December 2015 at: www.social-life.co/media/files/DESIGN_FOR_SOCIAL_SUSTAINABILITY_3.pdf

Woolcock, W and Narayan, D (2000) 'Social capital: implications for development theory, research and policy', *The World Bank Research Observer* 1 (15): 225–249.

World Bank (2014) 'Chapter 4: Cohesive and connected communities create resilience', *World Bank Development Report* (WDR), Washington DC: World Bank, 139-163, accessed on 6 December 2015 at: http://siteresources.worldbank.org/EXTNWDR2013/Resources/8258024-1352909193861/8936935-1356011448215/8986901-1380046989056/WDR-2014_Complete_Report.pdf

Zetter, R, Griffiths, D, Sigona, N, Flynn, D, Tauhid, P and Benyon, R (2006) *Immigration, Social Cohesion, and Social Capital: What are the Links*? London: Joseph Rowntree Foundation, accessed on 23 December 2015 at: www.jrf.org.uk/file/37076/download?token=VORkSS2P

4 Social sustainability and urban development

Linking social sustainability with urban development

This chapter considers how ideas of social sustainability have been translated into city frameworks and incorporated into urban design, and its influence on pro-community behaviours. By 2012, it was reported that in the preceding decade, governments, public agencies, policymakers, NGOs and corporations involved in urban planning policy and practice had become interested in applying the concept in the discourse on urban development, regeneration and housing in developed and developing regions (Karuppannan and Sivam, 2011; Woodcraft, 2012: 29). Powerful global institutions, such as the World Bank, the United Nations Environment Programme, European Investment Bank and European Bank for Reconstruction and Development developed programmes, policies and research addressing social sustainability in its own right (Woodcraft, 2012: 30). In our experience of discussions in the planning sector, these issues are often seen as 'softer', yet are harder to achieve. Operationalising social sustainability is an inherently political process. Examining how requires a closer look at who selects the dimensions operationalised, how such selections are justified, and the consequences for the physical structure of cities, and social activities taking place. Operationalisation can occur at policy or planning and design level, although there are often less than transparent processes that can make analysis of decision making difficult.

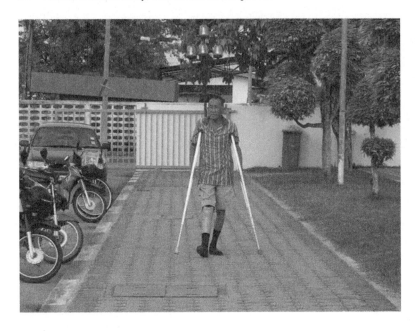

Figure 4.1 Yala Garden City HIA project
Source: HIA Division, Department of Health, Thailand.

City policies on social sustainability

In some cities and regions, policies have been devised that have, at times, incorporated social sustainability objectives and desired outcomes aiming to deliver broad benefits (see for example, Bramley and Power, 2009; Bramley *et al.*, 2009; Dempsey *et al.*, 2009; Karuppannan and Sivam, 2011; Weingaertner and Moberg, 2011; Woodcraft, 2012).

Vancouver, Canada

The Canadian city of Vancouver first adopted principles for environmental, economic, and social sustainability in 2002 (Cooper, 2006: iii). It then became the first city in the world to devise a social sustainability policy framework (Colantonio and Dixon, 2010: 15). Its goals were:

1   meeting residents' basic needs – including 'housing, health-care, food, jobs, income, and safety';

2   allowing residents to 'develop their personal capacity and fully participate in, contribute to, and benefit from all aspects of community';
3   that 'communities have a capacity to foster and support social inclusion on all dimensions and the positive development of all residents.' (Cooper, 2006: iii)

The second and third goals are pursuant through social resources: the individual's capacity to use their human capital for their and their community's well-being, and the social capital of the community.

The framework stressed the ability of a socially sustainable community to 'maintain and build on its own resources and have the resiliency to prevent and/or address problems in the future' (Cooper, 2006: 2).

UNESCO

UNESCO's MOST (Management of Social Transformations) programme compiled a series of ten large case studies in cities, and the social policies that determine social sustainability. The goal of achieving inclusive cities was attempted through a focus on city policies tackling governance; social and cultural policy; social infrastructure and public services; urban land and housing; urban transport and accessibility; and employment, economic revitalisation, and the building of inclusive public spaces (Stren and Polese, 2000).

Adelaide, Australia

In 2005, Adelaide City Council, Australia, signed a partnership agreement with the State Government of South Australia to make Adelaide socially sustainable. The policy's vision of a socially sustainable city was one that was 'equitable, diverse, connected, and democratic and provides a good quality of life'. Social sustainability was said to occur: 'when the formal and informal processes, systems, structures and relationships actively support the capacity of current and future generations to create vibrant, healthy and liveable cities.' The spotlight on 'structures and relationships' takes its framing from social capital. A policy framework was devised for the implementation of 'well-coordinated planning processes and implementation in the key areas of governance, housing, social inclusion and human services' (Adelaide City Council, 2005).

Urban planning, design and social sustainability

Policy frameworks that are supportive of urban social sustainability are key to legitimising concerns for it. However, within neighbourhoods at micro-level, the physical attributes of a city – urban form and design features, social infrastructure, and public spaces – can influence pro-community behaviours, as aspects of social capital and cohesion: social resources. For example, in the city of Guangzhou, China, the British design firm Arup reported on a scheme which aimed to encourage migrant workers to interact in public squares that were specifically re-designed to encourage socialising (Da Silva and Morera, 2014: 8). The scheme is not evaluated in their documentation. But as the project suggests, 'cities can and do help set the signals for engagement and interaction' (Kelly, 2012: 11). Too much social engineering may backfire, but a balanced approach to socially informed building development, 'socially aware planning', can send signals for pro-community behaviours.

Socially aware planning involves social objectives being incorporated into building or regeneration schemes with intentional positive impacts. Participatory or co-design approaches to development encourage essential community participation in the planning and design process (Sanoff, 2010), potentially creating or strengthening social capital and cohesion. Ideally, this approach sees collaboration between social scientists, planners, designers, and other physical environment specialists, along with 'normal' citizens, and integrates social science concepts and community concerns into the planning process. This requires openness to collaboration, and it is likely that training and capacity-building processes, both formal and less so, will need to prepare the ground and prepare practitioners for this challenging blend of social science, social policy, and design and planning skills and approaches. Chapters 6 and 7 offer 11 case studies from urban development projects and studies that show socially aware planning in practice. It is not a simple endeavour and depends on political will, and supportive policy and planning frameworks, as well as effective multi-stakeholder cooperation, and ideally professional skills that blend social science and policy with design and planning.

Socially aware planning in urban design

Jane Jacobs and William Hollingsworth Whyte were early advocates of design that integrates social groups and creates an active street life through 'varied and functional streetscapes' (Carpenter, 2013; Jacobs, 1961; Whyte, 1980). Meanwhile, the community design movement, emerging from the broader social movements of the 1960s, focused on the process of including community preferences into the design process to reflect grassroots inputs rather than merely top-down approaches (Lang, 1994). Formal planners and architects developed New Urbanism, a neo-traditionalist design movement whereby the built environment should prompt neighbourhood residents to interact, the fundamental premise of social capital, helping them develop a psychosocial sense of community (Talen, 1999: 1361).While sometimes criticised as elitist or naïve, it is widely taught in planning schools and strongly influences discussion and practice in this space (Bond and Thompson-Fawcett, 2007; Talen, 2000). Gehl (2006a, 2006b, 2010), in his books as well as his practice, has similarly focused on the importance of public space, and cities that are lively, safe, sustainable, and healthy. Some of these same elements emerge in Transit-Oriented-Development (TOD) approaches, originally expounded by Calthorpe (1993) and further expanded by Robert Cervero (1998) in work with his colleagues and students (for example, Suzuki, Cervero, and Iuchi, 2013). The design principles of New Urbanism are encapsulated in Table 4.1.

Whilst goal or dimension-oriented policy frameworks offer a vision for cities, development or regeneration at neighbourhood level can impact dynamic community social resources through reactive face-to-face interactions in local places and spaces. New Urbanist approaches are not the only ones building on these concepts and are sometimes criticised as noted above, but represent a major influence on designed projects in many places around the world. Moreover, while there are subtle differences, in broad measure, the people-oriented approaches mentioned earlier are consistent in their attention to detail in providing a designed built environment that is supportive of community bonds and interaction. In addition to designed developments, we also see organic growth and evolution

Table 4.1 The design principles of New Urbanism

Aspect of the neighbourhood	Design principles	Social goal
Architecture and site design	Shrinkage of private space; houses close to street; small parking lots and short distances from the street; porches face street; individuality in house design	Encouraging residents to leave their houses and interact in the public sphere
Density and scale	Small-scale, well-defined neighbourhoods with clear boundaries and a clear centre; increased residential density	Resident interaction leading to sense of community and neighbourliness
Streets	Viewed as public spaces; designed to encourage street life and increase in pedestrian activity; located in safe places	Pedestrian activity leading to feelings of safety, stronger community bonds and sense of place
Public space	Appropriate design and placement of public spaces such as parks and civic centres	Chance encounters between people, which strengthen community bonds; public spaces to be regarded as symbols of civic pride and sense of place, promoting community
Mixed land uses	A mixture of housing types; places of residence close to places to work, shop and recreate	Encourages lingering and repetitive chance encounters; facilitates social interaction of people of different incomes, races or ages; more walking and less driving; assists social integration, community bonds and sense of community

Adapted from: Talen (1999: 1363–1364)

of neighbourhoods incorporating some of these design aspects, often in informal settlements, and these should not be underappreciated or overlooked despite their distance from formal planned approaches (Appadurai, 2001; Hernandez-Garcia, 2013; Mitlin and Thompson,

1995). We must also acknowledge that the design emphasis of these approaches has often led to insufficient attention to equity, although currents are rumbling to remedy such inattention, at least in terms of the TOD area (ITDP, 2017; King *et al.*, 2017). These principles improve social sustainability in all contexts, although there is often room for continued improvement.

The UK social enterprise, *Social Life* (see case study in Chapter 7), coined the following definition of social sustainability that conjures up this union between the 'physical' and 'social', leading to quality of life and well-being. In italics is the part which is underpinned by social capital and cohesion:

Social sustainability is about people's quality of life, now and in the future. It describes the extent to which a neighbourhood supports individual and collective well-being. Social sustainability combines design of the physical environment with *a focus on how the people who live in and use a space relate to each other and function as a community.* It is enhanced by development that provides the right infrastructure to support a strong social and cultural life, opportunities for people to get involved, and scope for the place and the community to evolve (Bacon *et al.*, 2012: 9; Woodcraft, 2012: 35).

In addition, quality of life and well-being have been addressed in a report by the Australian think tank, the Grattan Institute. Their report *Social Cities* assembled a body of evidence attesting to the positive effects of urban 'social connections' between people – supported by effective design – on mental and physical health (Kelly, 2012).

Social sustainability and urban community behaviours

UK-based urban planning researchers found that the dimensions of social sustainability best promoted by urban form are indeed increased social capital and cohesion, and socio-economic equity and inclusion (Bramley and Power, 2009: 32). They devised a conceptual framework based on these concepts, broken into two strands: 'social equity' and 'sustainability of community' (Bramley *et al.*, 2009: 2126).

The 'social equity' strand focuses on 'access to services, facilities, and opportunities' (Bramley and Power, 2009: 32). The 'sustainability of community' strand concentrates on the 'continued viability, health and functioning' of 'community', the initial definition of social sustainability cited in Chapter 3 (Dempsey *et al.*, 2009: 290). This second strand is underpinned by social capital and cohesion. It itemises the 'collective aspects of social life' that are important at neighbourhood level with proven links to urban form (Dempsey *et al.*, 2009: 294). Whilst acknowledging the dependent relationship between these dual strands, and the importance of social equity – particularly in terms of people's access to 'good' neighbourhoods and facilities, and for cohesion, we focus on the 'sustainability of community' strand.

This strand is operationalised in the framework through measurable dimensions grounded in pro-community behaviours that are positive for, and contribute to social sustainability, a more supportive social environment, and improved quality of life for individuals and communities. Putting it in its context of social sustainability, we refer to our adaptation of this 'sustainability of community' framework as the 'socially sustainable community framework'. Itemised dimensions are our own in Table 4.2, alongside our analysis of their relationships to social capital and cohesion based on the literature cited in Chapter 3.

The items in this table are outcomes of an individual's experience of, and response to urban residence. The many ways in which one can influence another are covered in depth elsewhere (Dempsey *et al.*, 2009). We offer a summary explanation.

Living in a neighbourhood is the starting point for these behaviours and psychological responses. Social interaction is the basis for relationships between residents, and the emergence of social capital and cohesion. It is also the basis for social support provided by local network members, a crucial aspect of community resilience (discussed in Chapter 5). Social support influences feelings of safety and well-being (Dempsey *et al.*, 2009). Positive social interaction can also increase trust and reduce fears for safety on the streets – improving social cohesion. Individuals who are more socially isolated and do not participate may be less trusting and more fearful. Isolation may occur through choice or lack of choice, e.g. stigmatisation of people who experienced prejudice, physical immobility, lack of transport (or ability to pay for it) etc. Those who feel socially excluded may be less likely to develop pride in or attachment to their neighbourhood or community, or identify with either (Dempsey *et al.*, 2009: 294).

Social interaction with fellow dwellers and psychological satisfaction with one's home and a local environment can be at the heart of developing attachments. These signify enjoyment of life in a neighbourhood and give the individual a psychological sense of security. Any reduction in the quality of interactions or the attractiveness, functionality and congeniality of a physical location may lessen attachments, identifications and safety (Dempsey *et al.*, 2009: 296).

Social support, attachments to a community and place, feelings of safety and the experience of cohesive relationships can influence the

Table 4.2 The socially sustainable community framework

Dimension	Behavioural or psychological response	Relationships to social capital/social cohesion
Pride in and attachment to neighbourhood	Psychological	Place and community attachments: outcome of social capital
Social interaction within the neighbourhood	Individual interacting at group-level (group behaviour)	Component of social capital and social cohesion
Safety/security (versus risk of crime, antisocial behaviour)	Perception of safety: psychological	Indirect outcome of social capital via social support, social interaction, trust; driver for social cohesion
Perceived quality of local environment	Psychological	Relationships and attachments to place, related to sense of community: outcome of social capital
Satisfaction with the home	Psychological	Attachments to place and community: outcome of social capital
Stability (versus residential turnover)	Individual behaviour and community-level demographic change (or effects of migration)	Supports social capital and social cohesion; contributes to their emergence
Participation in collective group/civic activities	Individual behaviour	Outcome of social capital

Source: Adapted from Dempsey *et al.* (2009). The second and third columns are our analysis.

decision to stay in a place long-term. Equally, long-term residence can support social capital and cohesion, enhance safety, and reinforce attachments to places and communities (Dempsey *et al.*, 2009: 296; Oishi *et al.*, 2007: 831). Stability of community or low residential turnover has been linked to its sustainability, although it is not a given outcome (Dempsey *et al.*, 2009: 296). Long-term residence has been linked to a sense of belonging to a community and identifying with a place. These psychosocial attachments have been linked to pro-community behaviours (Oishi *et al.*, 2007: 832) such as participation in civic activities.

Participation in community and civic activities – a key outcome of social capital – brings people together in a potentially integrative context. It further reinforces attachments and the tendency to identify with a community (Dempsey *et al.*, 2009: 295) and its physical location. Conversely, having such attachments can promote willingness to participate in a community (Kearns and Forrest, 2000: 1001). Participation should ideally include giving the individual a say in how their area is developed. There are many reasons why people may not choose to participate – such as having social connections and interests elsewhere – which does not make their behaviour necessarily unsustainable. However, participation contributes to social sustainability (Dempsey *et al.*, 2009: 295).

We contend that built environment developments should promote these behaviours and psychological responses to contribute to social sustainability, bringing a 'human' perspective to urban planning and design. The framework has been applied to urban development research in India (Karuppannan and Sivam, 2011: 851). The behavioural and psychological dimensions are later compared to the dimensions of a similar framework proposed by Zautra, Hall, and Murray (2008: 143) for neighbourhood resilience, from which we also identified associated behaviours and psychological responses.

References

Adelaide City Council (2005) *Social Sustainability Partnership Agreement*, accessed on 23 December 2016 at: www.adelaidecitycouncil.com/assets/acc/Community/planning-programmes/docs/social_sustainability_partnership_agreement.pdf

Appadurai, A (2001) 'Deep democracy: urban governability and the horizon of politics', *Environment and Urbanization* 13(2): 23–43.

Bacon, N, Cochrane, D and Woodcraft, S (2012) *Creating Strong Communities: How to measure the social sustainability of new housing development*, Berkeley Housing Group, accessed on 23 December 2015 at: www.berkeleygroup.co.uk/media/pdf/7/8/berkeley-reports-and-opinions-social-sustainability-reports-creating- strong-communities-part-one.pdf

Bond, S and Thompson-Fawcett, M (2007) 'Public participation and New Urbanism: a conflicting agenda?', *Planning Theory and Practice* 8(4): 449–472.

Bramley, G and Power, S (2009) 'Urban form and social sustainability: the role of density and housing type', *Environment and Planning B: Planning and Design* 36: 30–48.

Bramley, G, Dempsey, N, Power, S, Brown, C and Watkins, D (2009) 'Social sustainability and urban form: evidence from Five British cities', *Environment and Planning A* 41: 2125–2142.

Calthorpe, P (1993) *The Next American Metropolis: Ecology, Community, and the American Dream*, New York: Princeton Architectural Press.

Carpenter, A (2013) *Resilience in the Social and Physical Realms: Lessons from the Gulf Coast*, Background Paper prepared for the *Global Assessment Report on Disaster Risk Reduction 2013*, Geneva: The United Nations Office for Disaster Risk Reduction (UNISDR) and Global Assessment Report on Disaster Risk Reduction (GAR), accessed on 6 December 2015 at: www. preventionweb.net/ english/hyogo/gar/2013/en/bgdocs/Carpenter,%202013.pdf

Cervero, R (1998) *The Transit Metropolis*. Washington, DC: Island Press.

Colantonio, A and Dixon, T (2010) *Urban Regeneration and Social Sustainability: Best Practice from European Cities*, Oxford: John Wiley & Sons.

Cooper, M (2006) *Social Sustainability in Vancouver*. Research Report F62. Ottawa: Family Network. Canadian Policy Research Networks, accessed on 23 December 2015 at: http://rcrpp.org/documents/45693_en.pdf

da Silva, J and Morera, B (2014) *City Resilience Index: City Resilience Framework*. Ove Arup and Partners International Limited and The Rockefeller Foundation, accessed on 23 December 2015 at: http://publications.arup.com/Publications/C/ City_Resilience_Framework.aspx

Dempsey, N, Bramley, G, Power, S and Brown, C (2009) 'The social dimension of sustainable development: defining urban social sustainability', *Sustainable Development* 19: 289–300.

Jacobs, J (1961) *The Death and Life of Great American Cities*, New York: Random House.

Gehl, J (2010) *Cities for People*, Washington DC: Island Press.

Gehl, J (2006a) *New City Life*, Copenhagen: The Danish Architectural Press.

Gehl, J (2006b) *Life between Buildings: Using Public Space*, Copenhagen: The Danish Architectural Press.

Hernandez-Garcia, J (2013) *Public Space in Informal Settlements: The Barrios of Bogota*, Newcastle upon Tyne, UK: Cambridge Scholars Publishing.

ITDP (2017) *TOD Standard 3.0*. Accessed on 15 September 2017 at: www.itdp.org/ library/standards-and-guides/tod3-0/

Karuppannan, S and Sivam, A (2011) 'Social sustainability and neighbourhood design: an investigation of residents' satisfaction in Delhi', *Local Environment: The International Journal of Justice and Sustainability* 16 (9): 849–870.

Kearns, A and Forrest, R (2000) 'Social cohesion and multilevel urban govern-ance', *Urban Studies* 37: 995–1017.

Kelly, J-F (2012) *Social Cities*, Melbourne: Grattan Institute, accessed on 22 December 2015 at: http://grattan. edu.au/report/social-cities/

King, R, Orloff, M, Virsilas, T and Pande, T (2017) 'Confronting the urban housing crisis in the global south: adequate, secure, and affordable housing', working paper chapter in *World Resources Report: Towards a More Equal City*, World Resources Institute.

Lang, J (1994) *Urban Design: The American Experience*, New York: John Wiley & Sons.

Mitlin D and Thompson, J (1995) 'Participatory approaches in urban areas: strengthening civil society or reinforcing the status quo', *Environment and Urbanization* 7(1): 231–250.

Oishi, S, Sherman, GD, Rothman, AJ, Snyder, M, Su, J, Zehm, K, Hertel, AW and Hope Gonzales, M (2007) 'The socioecological model of procommunity action: the benefits of residential stability', *Journal of Personality and Social Psychology* 95(3): 831–844.

Sanoff, H (2010) 'Democratic or Participatory Design: Introduction', *Democratic Design: Participation Case Studies in Urban and Small Town Environments*, Germany: VDM Verlag Dr. Muller.

Stren, R and Polese, M (2000) *The Social Sustainability of Cities: Diversity and the Management of Change*. Toronto: University of Toronto Press.

Suzuki, H, Cervero, R and Iuchi, K (2013) *Transforming Cities with Transit*, Washington DC: World Bank.

Talen, E (2000) 'New Urbanism and the culture of criticism', *Urban Geography* 21 (4), pp. 318–341.

Talen, E (1999) 'Sense of community and neighbourhood form: an assessment of the social doctrine of new urbanism', *Urban Studies* 36 (8): 1361–1379.

Weingaertner, C and Moberg, A (2011) 'Exploring social sustainability: learning from perspectives on urban development and companies and products', *Sustainable Development* 22 (2): 122–133.

Whyte, WH (1980) *The Social Life of Small Urban Spaces*, Washington DC: The Conservation Foundation.

Woodcraft, S (2012) 'social sustainability and new communities: Moving from concept to practice in the UK', *Procedia – Social and Behavioural Sciences* 68: 29–42.

Zautra, A, Hall, J and Murray, K (2008) 'Community development and community resilience: an integrative approach', *Community Development* 39 (3): 130–147.

5 Community resilience and environmental adversities

From socially sustainable to socially resilient communities

Many urban areas are populated by diverse individuals in criss-crossing networks, some of which may harbour social capital. Cohesive relationships within and between these networks are essential for successful collective cooperation. Social capital can also provide for more effective and quicker conflict resolution than more formal systems, allowing people and neighbourhoods to move beyond differences. New Urbanists and others have highlighted the features of urban form that may support the development of networks, but other variables that can also encourage or diminish social relationships – such as personal predisposition, conflict, crime and poverty – should also be addressed. A built environment that supports pro-community behaviours is conducive to community resilience to environmental adversities. We now discuss what is meant by community resilience.

What is community resilience?

> It appears that resilience is replacing sustainability in everyday discourse in much the same way as the environment has been subsumed in the hegemonic imperatives of climate change. Yet, it is not quite clear what resilience means, beyond the simple assumption that it is good to be resilient (Davoudi et al., 2012: 299).

This chapter reviews the concept of community resilience. The notion of resilience comes from physics and describes the action of a spring (CARRI, 2013: 2). Resilience as an aspect of an ecological system was first proposed by Holling (1973). 'Community resilience' is an idea that emanated from two different academic fields: socio-ecological systems theory (when a system is able to absorb shocks, sustain, renew and transform itself afterwards), and personal psychology and mental health (an individual's ability to recover from trauma) (Magis, 2010: 404). Combined in a community-level perspective, community resilience (sometimes also known as social resilience) (Adger, 2000), has been neatly defined as follows:

> the existence, development, and engagement of community resources by community members to thrive in an environment characterised by change, uncertainty, unpredictability, and surprise. Members of resilient communities intentionally develop personal and collective capacity that they engage to respond to and influence change, to sustain and renew the community, and to develop new trajectories for the communities' future.
>
> (Magis, 2010: 402)

There are many definitions and different disciplinary approaches to researching community resilience within academia (Cox and Perry, 2011: 395). This definition was selected on the strength of its match with our focus on social capital and its outcomes as resources for urban communities. Theories of community and social resilience have been targeted at people's ability to cope with environmental change (Adger, 2000) and natural disasters (McAslan, 2010: 1) among other types of crisis (e.g. terrorism and economic collapse). Our position on resilience is that everyday social sustainability sits on a continuum with resilience. Both centre on the shared and similar social resources that communities develop, and then harness quickly to respond to specific events. Resilience is therefore dynamic, resource-based, with fluctuating levels within communities.

Adaptive capacity

A community's background circumstances play some role in its 'adaptive capacity' for resilience, that is 'the capability of a particular system to effectively cope with shocks' (Martin-Breen and Anderies, 2011: 14). A community is a form of human system, so those in the community need the capacity to cope and respond effectively. Some communities are more vulnerable than others (Davis *et al.*, 2005; Magis, 2010: 405): for example, poor people living on riverbanks, floodplains, mountainsides or informal land prone to landslides or with little access to resources for recovery or political influence; people living alone without close family nearby; minorities; or those most vulnerable to poor health and well-being. 'Vulnerability' stems from a combination of exposure and sensitivity to hazards, and resources for coping. As our resilience case study from Khulna, Bangladesh will show, these factors made women more vulnerable to the effects of climate change than men. Adaptive capacity also has some place- and culture-specific characteristics (Adger, 2003: 400).

Overall resilience also depends on a community's combined ability to work towards a shared objective and influence resilience (Berkes and Ross, 2012: 6), the self-efficacy and agency of individuals and groups – their ability to take action – and the socio-demographic characteristics of the community (Berkes and Ross, 2012: 16). Increased exposure to unpredictable calamities may catalyse and develop communities' adaptive capacity to cope (Davis *et al.*, 2005; Magis, 2010: 405), but this is not always the case for communities with daily hardships. An effective community response may develop adaptive capacity, but may depend on pre-existing social resources. Community resilience works best in place-based communities although geographically dispersed networks may also be effective (Almedom, 2004; Berkes and Ross, 2012: 11; Maida, 2007). Resilience factors at individual, household, and community levels are interrelated and affect each other in non-linear ways (Berkes *et al.*, 2003; Berkes and Ross, 2012: 15).

Community resources and social capital

Communities cope best when their members have strong resources to help them develop adaptive capacity. Within the process of developing social capital, community members exhibit pro-community behaviours and/or psychological responses that are locally and culturally specific. Social process-based outcomes such as cohesion are also important (Berkes and Ross, 2012: 10). Social theories (Adger, 2000: 349; 2003: 395; McAslan, 2010; Magis, 2010: 405; Zautra, Hall, and Murray, 2008: 132) broadly agree that 'the capitals' – social, natural, human, cultural, built, financial, and political capital (see for example, DFID, 1999; Magis, 2010) – constitute the critical resources that can strengthen a community's resilience. Opinions diverge on which specific components are most useful, as these vary between communities (Berkes and Ross, 2012: 13). One set that has been identified is: 'People–place connections, values and beliefs, knowledge and learning, social networks, collaborative government, economic diversification and innovative economy, community infrastructure and support services, leadership and positive outlook; the built and natural environment, lifestyles, livelihoods' (Berkes and Ross, 2012: 11; 13–14; also see McAslan, 2010: 11; Zautra, Hall, and Murray, 2008: 138). As stated, we focus on social capital-related behaviours and psychological responses, as social strengths. Other dimensions of community resilience are covered elsewhere (for example, see World Bank, 2011; World Resources Institute, 2011). Adaptive capacity includes the capacity to develop and maintain social capital (Norris *et al.*, 2008, discussed in Cox and Perry, 2011: 396). Different social strengths are highlighted as important in resilience theories, such as social networks, communications, social support, inclusion and sense of belonging, as well as leadership (McAslan, 2010: 13), outlook on life including readiness to accept change, and learning (Berkes and Ross, 2012: 11). One study focuses on three social elements: social support, social participation, and community bonds (Norris *et al.*, 2008). Other work highlights social cohesion as the basis for the will and motivation for people to act resiliently together in the interests of their community (McAslan, 2010: 11; see also Chen, Liu, and Chan, 2006). Another list itemises relevant social science concepts: social capital, networks, sense of place, social identity, power (Berkes and Ross, 2012: 17).

The importance of these concepts is recognised but under-operationalised in the international planning sector. Michael Berkowitz, president of the USA-based Rockefeller Foundation's *100 Resilient Cities* network was asked in an interview to pinpoint the essence of the 'social and human infrastructure' of resilience. He stated that: 'social cohesion and social networks are often the key difference between more resilient and less resilient cities' (Goodyear, 2014). Trust among people in social networks and their ability to mobilise to work together and support each other collectively must be developed.

Yet resilience-building is a process, not an outcome (Berkes and Ross, 2012: 11). 'The capitals' – including social capital – and a community's unique strengths can increase/decrease in relation to the amount of 'investment' in them (Magis, 2010: 410). When they are mobilised and strengthened, they perform better, are more effective in times of crisis, and assist in the development of new resources (Magis, 2010: 406).

The more resources a community has to draw on and the more it strives to increase them, the greater its resilience will be (Magis, 2010: 406). City-level Resilience Strategies should monitor changes in the social capital-derived strengths that contribute to resilience for any downturns that may impact on adaptive capacity and quality of life (Zautra, Hall, and Murray, 2008: 143). Urban and community development must help a community to conserve and reinforce its social strengths.

Environmental adversity and the resilient urban community

This section explains why and how people turn to their immediate contacts and depend upon supportive built environments after a disaster. Urban communities in cities worldwide are already impacted by climate change and know they face increased risk in the future. The C40, a network of megacities around the globe collaborating to address climate change, reported that 76 per cent of city respondents to its survey believe that climate change could threaten businesses in their cities (AECOM for CDP/Bloomberg Philanthropies and C40 Cities, 2014). They are increasingly subjected to unpredictable rainfall patterns, sea level rise, and wider and less predictable temperature extremes (World Bank, 2010). Such events damage the physical and social infrastructure, restrict or prevent access to essential economic and environmental resources, and disrupt the lives of and displace many people resulting in significant social, health and well-being impacts. When a negative environmental event – high temperatures, a storm, cyclone, typhoon or hurricane, flood, earthquake and so on – inflicts damage on, and disrupts routines in an urban community, people turn first to their social networks of relatives, family and neighbours for support (Bidwell and Dell, 2011: 4; Klinenberg, 2013: 4). A multi-country study of poor people – *Voices of the Poor* – conducted by the World Bank revealed that 'across locales, respondents consider kin, family, and community-based and religious organisations among the most effective support systems' (World Bank, 2013: 154).

Displaced people turn immediately to available urban spaces to meet their accommodation and organisational needs in a flexible way. Residents of the Chilean city of Concepción and its Metropolitan Area were hit by a colossal earthquake on 27 February 2010, followed by four tsunami waves that lashed the nearby coast. People rapidly sought safety and established temporary encampments and community meeting places in the area's network of 'squares, parks, vacant lots and undeveloped spaces' (Allan *et al.*, 2013: 250).

This and another example crystallises the connection between social capital and urban form and space during environmental crises. In 1995, a heatwave struck Chicago, USA, killing 739 people, including many elderly (World Bank, 2013: 139). The neighbourhoods where people fared better had in common a physical environment that was conducive to networks, and established relationships within neighbourhood networks. A Latino community living in crowded apartments and densely packed streets knew their neighbours. The availability of shops, stores, restaurants and community organisations brought people into contact with neighbours and friends, with whom they participated in block parties and church groups. They knocked on neighbours' doors to check up on their well-being (Klinenberg, 2013: 4). For some, neighbourhood social capital meant the difference between life and death.

Those living within close physical proximity are the nearest at hand to help with caring for affected people, re-establishing community organisation and motivating community spirit, stabilising and repairing physical damage, and other resilient actions. People's ability to work together – drawing on their existing social capital and cohesive relationships – becomes all the more important. A socially sustainable community may also be a resilient community (McAslan, 2010: 7–8; Zautra, Hall, and Murray, 2008: 132).

Creating community resilience through community development

This section outlines formal approaches to developing community social resources for resilience. Analysts and policymakers recommend capacity-strengthening community development initiatives during times of calm and after a crisis (Thornley *et al.*, 2013: 34), which can improve diverse communities' routine lives, create adaptive capacity and highlight 'agency' in preparation for acting resiliently during crises. Both the UK and US governments, for example, have recognised that resilience depends on 'effective collective action and local organisation *before* a crisis develops' (Bach *et al.*, 2010). The community development approach to increasing adaptive capacity identifies some key principles, laid out in the text box below.

Key community development principles for increasing adaptive capacity

- A focus on a community's resources not deficits (Zautra, Hall, and Murray, 2008: 138)
- Emphasising the community's own knowledge of itself to help identify its strengths, and strategise capacity-building interventions (Magis, 2010: 405)
- Social learning and capacity-building opportunities are important for building community strengths and relationships (Berkes and Ross, 2012: 13; 17; Goldstein, 2009)
- Participatory projects – such as improving a neighbourhood – that allocate collective tasks to help people build on their self-organising capacities, to bond as a community, and create cohesion and a sense of community are a useful tool for building resilience (Berkes and Ross, 2012: 16)
- Capacity-building projects should recognise that resilience can be exclusionary when decisions are made over whose resilience to strengthen and whose not to (Davoudi *et al.*, 2012: 306). Initiatives should ensure inclusivity of all individuals and social groups.

Community resilience and urban community behaviours

This section introduces a framework on resilient community behaviours. Resilience theories have linked social capital, cohesion and community resilience. But what are the pro-community behaviours that contribute to a community's resilience? A review of 22 academic papers from the health and community development literature prepared by a US-based research team identified the dimensions making up the 'fundamentals of neighbourhood resilience' (Zautra, Hall and Murray, 2008: 143).[1] We refer to our slight adaptation of this framework as the 'resilient neighbourhood community framework.' Other work offers less comprehensive lists (see for example, McAslan, 2010). In Table 5.1, we identify how these dimensions relate to social capital and cohesion, as either component, outcome, or as closely related to the dimensions of social sustainability, based on our literature reviews of these concepts.

Four dimensions are shared between the two frameworks, 'socially sustainable community' and 'resilient neighbourhood community',

Table 5.1 The resilient neighbourhood community framework

Dimensions of a resilient neighbourhood community	Behaviour or psychological response	Relationship to social capital, social cohesion, social sustainability
Neighbours that trust one another	Psychological	Cognitive social capital
Neighbours that interact on a regular basis	Active behaviour	Desired outcome of social capital; aspect of social cohesion, social sustainability
Residents who own their own houses and stay for a while [or rental tenants or informal settlement dwellers that reside in an area for the long-term.]*	Individual and community-level behaviour (economic and social behaviours)	Social sustainability
Residents with a sense of community	Psychological	Desirable outcome of social capital, closely related to social sustainability
Social cohesion	Social process with behavioural and psychological dimensions	Desirable outcome of social capital, closely related to social sustainability
Residents who work together for the common good and are involved in community events	Active behaviour	Social cohesion; desirable outcome of/closely related to social capital
Formal and informal places for civic gathering	Physical dimension	Desirable feature of the built environment in New Urbanism

* The sentence in square brackets is our addition. We recognise that although home ownership is seen as desirable in the British context from which this framework emerged, length of residence is the important variable internationally where other residential arrangements occur. For example, in parts of Continental Europe, long-term rental tenancies are the norm.

illuminating the overlap between the social resources required. These are outlined in Table 5.2.

These two frameworks are applied in our case studies in Chapters 6–8 to investigate how applicable they are in real urban development projects.

Table 5.2 Shared dimensions of socially sustainable, resilient communities

Socially sustainable community	Resilient neighbourhood community
Pride and attachment to the neighbourhood	Sense of community (also an affective feeling of local belonging)
Social interaction within the neighbourhood	Neighbours that interact on a regular basis
Stability versus residential turnover	Residents who own their own houses and stay for a while [or rental tenants or informal settlement dwellers that reside in an area for the long-term]
Participation in collective group/ civic activities	Residents who work together for the common good and are involved in community events

Note

1 It is not clear whether any of the papers Zautra *et al.* reviewed were taken from non-USA contexts, but we test these dimensions on projects from other countries.

References

Adger, WN (2000) 'Social and ecological resilience: are they related?', *Progress in Human Geography* 24: 347–64.

Adger, WN (2003) 'Social capital, collective action, and adaptation to climate change', *Economic Geography* 79 (4): 387–404.

AECOM for CDP/Bloomberg Philanthropies and C40 Cities (2014) *Protecting our Capital: how Climate Adaptation in Cities Creates a Resilient Place for Business*, accessed on 23 December 2015 at: www.cdp.net/CDPResults/CDP-global-cities-report-2014.pdf.

Allan, P, Byant, M, Wirsching, C, Garcia, D and Rodriguez, MT (2013) 'The influence of urban morphology on the resilience of cities following an earthquake', *Journal of Urban Design* 18 (2): 242–262.

Almedom, A (2004) 'Factors that mitigate war-induced anxiety and mental distress', *Journal of Biosocial Science* 36: 445–461.

Bach, R, Doran, R, Gibb, L, Kaufman, D and Settle, K (2010) Policy Challenges in Supporting Community Resilience, Working Paper for the Multinational Community Resilience Policy Group (Co-chaired by US and UK), London, accessed on 6 December at: www.fema.gov/media-library/assets/documents/21050?id=4563

Berkes, F and Ross, H (2012) 'Community resilience: toward an integrated approach', *Society and Natural Resources: An International Journal* 26 (1): 5–20.

Berkes, F, Colding, J and Folke, C (2003) *Navigating Social–Ecological Systems: Building Resilience for Complexity and Change*, Cambridge: Cambridge University Press.

Bidwell, S and Dell, R (2011) *Long-term Planning for Recovery after Disasters: Ensuring Health in All Policies*, Christchurch, NZ: Canterbury District Health Board. accessed on 22 December 2015 at: www.cph.co.nz/files/LTPRecovery-HIAP-fulldocument.pdf

CARRI (2013) *Definitions of Community Resilience: An Analysis*, A CARRI Report, Community and Regional Resilience Institute, accessed on 23 December 2015 at: www.resilientus.org/wp-content/uploads/2013/08/definitions-of-community-resilience.pdf

Chen, LC, Liu, YC and Chan, KC (2006) 'Integrated community-based disaster management programme in Taiwan: a case study of Shang-An Village', *Natural Hazards* 37 (1–2): 209–223.

Cox, RS and Perry, KE (2011) 'Like a fish out of water: reconsidering disaster recovery and the role of place and social capital in community disaster resilience', *American Journal of Community Psychology* 48: 395–411.

Davis, R, Cook, D and Cohen, L (2005) 'A community resilience approach to reducing ethnic and racial disparities in health', *American Journal of Public Health* 95 (12): 2168–2173.

Davoudi, S, Shaw, S, Haider, JL, Quinlan, AE, Peterson, GD, Wilkinson, C, Fünfgeld, H, McEvoy, D, Porter, L and Davoudi, S (2012) 'Planning theory and practice interacting traps: resilience assessment of a pasture management system in Northern Afghanistan, Urban Resilience: what does it mean in planning practice?, Resilience as a useful concept for climate change adaptation? The politics of resilience for planning: a cautionary note', *Planning Theory & Practice* 13(2): 299–333.

DFID (1999) *Sustainable Livelihoods Guidance Sheets*. Department for International Development, Government of the United Kingdom, accessed during 2014 at: http:// www.efls.ca/webresources/DFID_Sustainable_livelihoods_guidance_sheet.pdf

Goldstein, B (2009) 'Resilience to surprises through communicative planning', *Ecology and Society* 14 (20): article 33. accessed on 23 December 2015 at: www.ecologyandsociety.org/vol14/iss2/art33

Goodyear, S (2014) 'How to help the world's cities prepare for the next disaster: a conversation with 100 Resilient Cities president Michael Berkowitz', *Citylab* website, accessed on 6 December 2015 at: www.citylab.com/politics/2014/09/how-to-help-the-worlds-cities-prepare-for-the-next-disaster/380808/

Holling, CS (1973) 'Resilience and the stability of ecology systems', *Annual Review of Ecology and Systematics* 4: 1–23.

Klinenberg, E (2013) 'Adaptation: how can cities be "climate proofed"?', *Dept of Urban Planning. The New Yorker Digital edition* 7th of January 2013, accessed on 22 December 2015 at: www.newyorker.com/magazine/2013/01/07/adaptation-2

Magis, K (2010) 'Community resilience: an indicator of social sustainability', *Society & Natural Resources: An International Journal* 23 (5): 402–426.

Maida, CA (2007) *Sustainability and communities of place*. New York: Berghahn.

Martin-Breen, P and Anderies, JM (2011) *Resilience: A Literature Review*, Brighton, UK: Bellagio Initiative: IDS, accessed on 6 December 2015 at: http://opendocs.ids.ac.uk/opendocs/handle/123456789/3692#.VmOFQ7_-oWc

McAslan, A (2010) *Community Resilience: Understanding the Concept and its Application*. Australia: Torrens Resilience Institute, accessed on 22 December 2015 at: http://sustainablecommunitiessa.files.wordpress.com/2011/06/community-resilience-from-torrens-institute.pdf

Norris, F, Stevens, S, Pfefferbaum, B, Wyche, K and Pfefferbaum, R (2008) 'Community resilience as a metaphor, theory, set of capacities, and strategy for disaster readiness', *American Journal of Community Psychology* 41 (1–2): 1573–2770.

Thornley, L, J Ball, L Signal, K Lawson-Te Aho, E Rawson (2013), *Building Community Resilience: Learning from the Canterbury earthquakes*, Report prepared for Health Research Council and Canterbury Medical Research Foundation, Christchurch, accessed on 6 December 2015 at: www.quigleyandwatts.co.nz/research- and-analysis/Building_Community_Resilience_report-March_2013.pdf?final2

World Bank (2010) *Cities and Climate Change: An Urgent Agenda*. The World Bank Urban Development Series Knowledge Papers, Volume 10. (especially Part II), Washington DC: World Bank, accessed on 6 December 2015 at: http://siteresources.worldbank.org/INTUWM/Resources/340232-1205330656272/CitiesandClimateChange.pdf

World Bank (2011) *Economics of Adaptation to Climate Change*, accessed on 23 December 2015 at: www-wds.worldbank.org/external/default/WDSContentSer ver/WDSP/IB/2012/0 6/27/000425970_20120627163039/Rendered/PDF/702670ESW0P10800EACCSynthesisReport.pdf

World Bank (2013) Brief: Social Inclusion, August 15, 2013, accessed 3 January 2016 at: www.worldbank. org/en/topic/socialdevelopment/brief/social-inclusion

World Resources Institute (2011) *World Resources Report 2010-2011, Decision Making in a Changing Climate: Adaptation Challenges and Choices*, accessed on 23 December 2015 at: http://pdf.wri.org/world_resources_report_2010-2011.pdf

Zautra, A, Hall, J and Murray, K (2008) 'Community development and community resilience: an integrative approach', *Community Development* 39 (3): 130–147.

6 Creating built environments that influence pro-community behaviours

How does the built environment influence people?

Chapters 6 and 7 explore the pro-community behaviours (dimensions) from the 'socially sustainable community' framework (Bramley and Power, 2009; and Dempsey, Bramley, Power and Brown, 2009) that real development projects can influence, and any new dimensions found in these projects. Eleven case studies are presented in total. Some of these: Delhi (1), Cape Town (1), Belfast (1), southern England (1), Portland (1) and Manchester (1) are split up, and parts of them are discussed under four different stages of the socially aware planning process (see Chapter 7) where they were considered to provide useful examples of more than one stage. Chapter 6 showcases the core influence of the built environment on pro-community behaviours in two case studies. The first, from Buenos Aires, Argentina, explores how a community contested developer plans in order to maintain social strengths. The second, from Delhi, India, itemises aspects of urban form that influence pro-community behaviours with broader consequences.

Case study: Housing expansion in Buenos Aires, Argentina

Caballito is a middle-class neighbourhood (*barrio*) in central Buenos Aires, Argentina (case based on Caistor, 2013). Its streets feature elegant one- or two-storey houses reminiscent of old European architecture that were built around the turn of the twentieth century. Constructed on narrow plots of land in rows along blocks (*cuadras*), street layouts were created that influenced pro-community outcomes: residents came to know their neighbours (*active behaviour*), and felt safe (*psychological response*). These properties were built on the city's grid system, in walking distance of amenities and connected to the city centre. Sadly, some have been demolished following intense demands for land resulting from economic boom, and the accompanying easing of planning regulations since 2005 for investment-led development.

Typically, developers buy undervalued plots accommodating these homes, demolish them, and construct luxury residential towers for affluent incomers. The towers are usually between 10 and 30 storeys high, and include private parking, sports and other facilities. They are set back without open or active ground floors providing life, activity, and eyes on the street. New residents are cut off from spontaneous social encounters with neighbours from the older dwellings. The self-contained towers provide no reason for residents to seek social connections outside the home. The terraced houses were usually built butting right up against the street, and became physically joined over time as more families bought adjacent plots and built homes that created more apparent physical connections than those in the apartment buildings (Figure 6.1).

Some longer-term inhabitants of Caballito experienced feelings of insecurity due to the appearance of these isolationist and highly securitised residences, and the fact that incomers from a different socio-economic group were intentionally segregating themselves from the wider community. These are both negative social impacts threatening to

Figure 6.1 Terraced house amid tower blocks, Caballito, Buenos Aires
Source: Lucia Caistor-Arendar.

weaken social capital and cohesion among existing networks of residents. The changed physical environment prompted insecurity (*psychological response*), and the enactment of defiant pro-community behaviours (*behavioural response*). Residents drew upon their existing social relationships to mobilise themselves collectively to campaign. They formed groups such as Proto Comuna Caballito, SOS Caballito, and joined city-wide groups such as Basta de Demoler! (Stop the Demolitions!).The residents campaigned successfully against the easing of regulations. It was argued that the neighbourhood's infrastructure was overstretched due to densification. This can be a chicken and egg situation where infrastructure can be provided in advance of, or in response to a growing population. However, in Caballito, its overextended capacity was proved by a negative audit of the availability of water infrastructure such as sewers that the local government were forced to commission. The campaign resulted in a new law – 2722 – being passed by the Legislation of Urban Development. It restricted the height of future towers in three zones in Caballito, rendering their construction economically impractical for developers. The campaign brought existing residents even closer together, enhancing their bonds, agency/capacity to act, and hence, social capital.

Case study: Public open spaces in Delhi, India

Ideas of social sustainability are also of interest in developing countries. Indian researchers Karuppannan and Sivam (2011) have explored these issues in Delhi, India, applying the 'sustainability of community' framework created by Bramley and Power (2009) and Dempsey *et al.* (2009). They mixed qualitative with quantitative methods (see Chapter 7) to explore the influence of neighbourhood urban form, particularly public open spaces, on residents' social interactions and participation in neighbourhood activities in two suburbs, Dwarka sub-city and Sukdev Vihar. The Delhi Development Authority constructed all the buildings in the same period for residents with similar socio-economic demographic profiles but used varying design form. Three sites (1–3) were explored, two (1–2) in Dwarka sub-city, and one (3) in Sukdev Vihar via resident interviews.

Sites 1 and 3 had apartments in high-rise (1) or four-storey blocks (3), with dwelling units set around the public realm or semi-public open space, or (1) located near to better, more diverse, and well-located public spaces. Site 2 had more four-storey terraced housing blocks containing individual units facing paved roads and near to linear semi-public open spaces.

At sites 1 and 3, mixed land use and easily accessible semi-public and public open spaces positively impacted social integration/inclusion, people's relationships with neighbours, and feelings of safety. The close proximity of dwelling units and nearby buildings led to residents' knowing each other by name and becoming friends. Lively streets and well-situated public spaces contributed to safety and security in the whole area. The well-utilised physical spaces created social places where people participated in formal and informal social gatherings. All these effects raised residents' satisfaction with the neighbourhood, and influenced pride and attachments to the place.

At site 2, the terraced housing and linear semi-public open spaces negatively impacted on the frequency and quality of residents' interaction with neighbours. People did not perceive the open spaces to be well located or to encourage informal or formal interaction, and also blamed the neighbourhood's design. Fewer people participated in social gatherings. Overall, they were less satisfied with the neighbourhood than people living at sites 1 and 3. Fewer individuals felt pride in or expressed attachments to place. The street-facing buildings did generate feelings of safety, however, and adults walked and children played there due to the lack of proper open spaces.

Table 6.1 shows the researchers' findings: specific aspects of urban form influenced pro-community behaviours. These can have direct effects on individuals' psychosocial health and well-being, and on positive community-level social processes, such as the formation of social capital or cohesion, or occurrence of social inclusion, which contribute to social sustainability. We analysed these in the third and fourth columns of Table 6.1.

This case also illuminated the role of cultural norms in mediating the impacts of aspects of urban form that promote social sustainability in each context. In these Delhi neighbourhoods, it was culturally acceptable for people to greet each other in public, thus this norm played a role in facilitating human contact. In some cities in Northern Europe, it is less of a common cultural norm to greet neighbours, even if they live close by and have a visible presence in the public realm.

Norms can be changed, sometimes by design, but are sometimes too deeply ingrained for a rapid shift. The social impacts of physical features are also context-specific. In Delhi, homes joined together in rows were not conducive to neighbourly relations whereas in Caballito, Buenos Aires, this aspect of urban form had the opposite effect.

Table 6.1 Influence of urban form on pro-community outcomes and social processes

Aspects of urban form	Influence on pro-community behaviours	Individual and community level 'social process' outcomes		Nature of impact	
Mixed land use and mixed housing developments	• Promotes interaction across socio-economic and age groups • Promotes visibility of diverse social groups	1 2	Social inclusion/ integration Builds bridging social capital	1 2	Social process Social process
Public open spaces	• Promotes periodic interaction and social relationships – with neighbours and area residents – leading to formation of social ties	1 2 3 4	Builds social capital and cohesion Promotes psychosocial sense of place and community Promotes satisfaction with neighbourhood Enhances well-being	1 2 3 4	Social process Individual and group level psychosocial response Psychological response Positive effect on mental and physical health
Semi-public open spaces	• Promotes regular interaction and social relationships – with neighbours – leading to formation of social ties	1 2 3 4	Builds social capital and cohesion Promotes psychosocial sense of place and community Promotes satisfaction with neighbourhood Enhances well-being	1 2 3 4	Social process Individual and group level psychosocial response Psychological response Positive effect on mental and physical health
Cluster housing	• Close proximity of dwellings and windows promotes social interaction	1 2	Builds social capital and cohesion Promote psychosocial sense of place and community	1	Individual and group level psychosocial response
Row/ terraced housing	• Restricts social interaction to next door neighbours	1	Limits development of social capital, psychosocial sense of place and community, satisfaction with neighbourhood; adverse effects on well-being	1	Individual and group level psychosocial response

(Adapted from Karuppannan and Sivam, 2011)

(a)

(b)

Figure 6.2 (a) Cluster housing (b) Terraced housing, Dwarka sub-city, Delhi
Source: Alpana Sivam.

References

Bramley, G and Power, S (2009) 'Urban form and social sustainability: the role of density and housing type', *Environment and Planning B: Planning and Design* 36: 30–48.

Caistor, L (2013) 'Losing the plot in Buenos Aires', *The Social Life of Cities: Stories about Urban Innovation*, London: Social Life, accessed on 22 December 2015 at: www.social-life.co/publication/Social_Life_of_Cities_stories/

Dempsey, N, Bramley, G, Power, S and Brown, C (2009) 'The social dimension of sustainable development: Defining urban social sustainability', *Sustainable Development* 19: 289–300.

Karuppannan, S and Sivam, A. (2011) 'Social sustainability and neighbourhood design: an investigation of residents' satisfaction in Delhi', *Local Environment: The International Journal of Justice and Sustainability* 16 (9): 849–870.

7 Built environments that influence socially sustainable behaviours

The four stages of socially aware planning for an urban development

Chapter 7 looks at the marriage of physical and social factors in a 'socially planned urban development process' through nine more urban projects. These case studies navigate us through the process of developing and implementing a built environment scheme, and offer examples of approaches, methods and tools that can be employed over four stages to meet social objectives and create immediate[1] positive social impacts. Stage 1 includes well-established development stages where financial and legal concerns prevail, that typically do not include 'social' aspects. Cases discussed at this stage show how social objectives are conceptualised into schemes. We are aware that the stages as presented here are quite different from those typical of urban development. Much of what real estate and urban development specialists typically do is included in Stage 1.[2] However, we believe that looking at the entire life cycle of the project, from conception to use, is essential to understanding the social dynamics beyond mere design. The pro-community behaviours that each project influenced are summarised at the end of this chapter. The stages, along with recommended steps and actions, are summarised in Table 7.1.

This process incorporates principles from a social or health impact assessment (SIA and HIA) (Cave, 2015; Vanclay, 2002) such as community involvement, matching data on community needs and strengths with project benefits, and monitoring and evaluation. Differentially, our process begins from a scheme's earliest conception,[3] and follows the entire development. We stress depth of investigation at Stage 2, and that social and cultural data explicitly informs design decisions at Stage 3.

Table 7.1 The four stages of urban development for social sustainability

Stage of an urban development	Actions recommended for urban development teams
Stage 1: Scheme Conception; Land Acquisition, Finance, Consistency with Broader Land Use, and Predevelopment (often broadly referred to as Real Estate Predevelopment)	Defining a vision – practical, financial, and social – for a development. To emphasise social sustainability, the social vision and social objectives to enhance communities' social resources and strengths as well as traditional analysis of needs, opportunities, and potential solutions through plans/designs should be emphasised. However, it is the second part of this stage – the traditional real estate pre-development process, itself a multi-stage process – that generally gets the most attention.
Stage 2: Research and Community Participation	Using appropriate strategies and methods to: 1) uncover the social and cultural context and community dynamics to inform sensitive planning decisions; 2) explore the needs, social resources and strengths of a community with their participation to produce relevant designs.
Stage 3: Design Decisions and Implementation	Using social and cultural information to inform design decisions about the characteristics of buildings or public spaces: placement, layout, form and aesthetics; ensuring social input in implementation, along with more traditional inputs and analysis.
Stage 4: Monitoring and Evaluation	Monitoring and assessing social input and social impacts, along with more traditional inputs and analysis.

Stage 1: scheme conception: incorporating social objectives

Built environment developments can be conceptualised and planned to identify and meet the social needs, and enhance the social resources and strengths of residents and users, as well as benefiting developers, and the local economy. Visions and plans for schemes can factor in building and strengthening the pro-community behavioural and psychological dimensions of social sustainability through the influences of space and place. The projects discussed in this chapter meet some of these aims.

Volatile urban contexts: Cape Town, South Africa; and Belfast, Northern Ireland, UK

Cities with a volatile social history of division and poverty, or more peaceful and prosperous cities both benefit from urban settlements that integrate diverse resident groups, are safe, and promote community social resources, strengths and well-being. We first highlight building and regeneration projects in Cape Town, South Africa and Belfast, Northern Ireland (UK) that have initially conceptualised these objectives into their plans. Both have been blighted by chequered histories of painful division and segregation – South Africa's enforced racial apartheid, and Northern Ireland's long-standing sectarian conflict. The example of a UK housing developer, operating in southern England, shows that once stable societal conditions exist, and basic safety, cohesion, and economic opportunities are established, standards for quality of life, well-being and social sustainability can be raised. Apartheid-era spatial planning segregated whites from non-whites in Cape Town's centre and peripheries. Its central railway station (Fataar and Petzer, 2014) symbolised injustice. Built in 1966, it combined two separate stations – one for white and one for non-white commuters. City residents would pass in spatial proximity to each other without ever meeting. Segregated suburbs meant that post-apartheid city planners needed to consider the spatial reintegration of residential areas. The country's high rates of violence and crime resulted in gated communities threatening to compound contemporary segregation. Poor Black communities remain on the geographic and economic periphery in places such as Khayelitsha, a partially informal township in Western Cape (VPUU website).[4] Two schemes planned to tackle the spatial and economic marginalisation of poor Black Africans, and build safer, more cohesive communities.

Central Railway Station, Cape Town, South Africa

The 2010 World Cup provided the City of Cape Town with a deadline for renovating apartheid-era architecture to reflect its new democratic ideals. The City appointed Khalied Jacobs, a partner at Cape Town's Jakupa Architects in collaboration with Makeka Design Lab, to redesign the central station's features to support the inclusion of the city's poorest and most working-class residents. This was a bid to reclaim the space. A public space on the roof allowed informal vendors to sell produce and services to commuters. Resting areas with grass and trees outside the station allowed people to gather, sleep and even beg. The station is located near informal settlements – offering low-income people a central place to congregate – and has become like a city square. Plans exist to overhaul five more railway stations, and create public squares to promote inclusion. Social inclusion is closely linked to social sustainability and a desired outcome of social capital.

Violence Prevention through Urban Upgrading (VPUU), Khayelitsha, Cape Town, South Africa

Khayelitsha has been subject to renovation through the City of Cape Town's Violence Prevention through Urban Upgrading Programme (VPUU). Densely populated – with 200,000 families occupying 6 square km, 90.5 per cent of its inhabitants are low-income Black Africans. They lived in matchbox-style houses with access to basic infrastructure. Before the scheme, the urban environment was decrepit with undignified public space, a lack of street lighting, informal roads and pavements, and there were frequent crimes such as murders, rapes, robberies, and domestic violence against women and children. The VPUU sought to help the community make the township vibrant, safer and more attractive; community life more peaceful, harmonious and of better quality; and also, environmentally, economically and socially sustainable (Figure 7.1).

In Belfast, the urban landscape has come to symbolise divisions in a more organic way (Pharoah, Norman and Hale, 2007). Many decades of sectarian violence between Protestants and Catholics have resulted in a

Figure 7.1 Belfast mural
Source: Will Norman.

culturally territorialised urban landscape. City spaces, aspects of urban form, and travel routes are adopted as the territory or symbol of either side, or as neutral. High walls topped with wire mesh (so-called 'peace walls') separate some neighbourhoods. Murals painted on buildings, flags, memorials and street furniture all mark invisible territorial barriers or borders. Maps, streets and their names, painted curb stones, graffitied slogans, and buildings are all symbolic, and walking and driving routes are characterised as belonging to one side or the other.

Urban developers have high potential to encroach on significant markers unaware, and contribute to tensions. There are, however, ways of using the neutral spaces to attempt integration, offering the potential for social cohesion. A positive approach was taken by a private developer who wished to build a new mixed housing complex on a former industrial site for younger tenants, with fewer years of exposure to the sectarian horrors. From the outset, the objective was integration for Protestants and Catholics living there, using the facilities, and passing through the site to access the city centre.

Peaceful urban context: southern England, UK

Another example shows how building developments in more peaceful, prosperous and cohesive cities are conceived of to promote social capital and cohesion directly. The Berkeley Group, a private UK housing developer, builds new 'housing communities' (housing estates) where residents live in close proximity. The developer wished to improve their understanding of the relationship between physical and social factors as they did not know whether its previous settlements had enhanced residents' social strengths or thrived long term. Berkeley wished to build homes that promoted quality of life, well-being and hence social sustainability, and simply make living in them more enjoyable. They set out to marry the physical form and social infrastructure of developments with residents' social needs.

Social objectives

Social objectives were woven into each scheme's vision and aims. These are:

1   redressing the spatial marginalisation and promoting social and economic inclusion of the poor (*Cape Town Railway Station, Cape Town, South Africa*);
2   making a poor township vibrant, safer and more attractive; community life more peaceful, harmonious and of better quality; and

ultimately environmentally, economically and socially sustainable (*VPUU in Khayelitsha, Cape Town, South Africa*);
3   integrating Catholics and Protestants divided by sectarian conflict (*Housing Complex, Belfast, Northern Ireland, UK*);
4   improving residents' quality of life, well-being and social sustainability (*The Berkeley Group, southern England, UK*).

Stage 2: research and community participation

Careful scoping research is needed to understand the social and cultural context, and existing community dynamics into which a development will be inserted once a social vision and objectives for a scheme have been defined. Context and dynamics will impact on the way that developers approach a community, as in Belfast. A community's existing social resources, strengths, and needs (and weaknesses) must be mapped using the expertise of social scientists to meet social sustainability (and resilience) objectives. Community members' local knowledge and experience should be harnessed through their participation to democratise decision making about designs that affect them (Fagence, 1977; King, 1983; Sanoff, 2010), to empower them, and to inform better designs for commercial advantage. Our case studies offer different ways of working with researchers and communities, and methods of gathering this information.

Mapping the cultural meanings of urban space: Belfast, Northern Ireland, UK

The physical environment cannot be understood simply by looking at it. Mapping the social and cultural meanings of city spaces and the memories they provoke in fragile urban contexts helps to locate and shape the design of buildings and public spaces in a sensitive manner. The Belfast developer hired anthropologists to research local meanings by engaging both Catholics and Protestants, thus safeguarding its plans. It was important that the developer grasped the sometimes tense and uneasy social dynamics between residents, and understood the limits of mixing in the so-called neutral spaces.[5] Social research methods were used over just 4 weeks in 2007 to generate ethnographic data. These included: meeting the design team, a workshop with community leaders to elicit local information, focus groups with residents under and over 35, participant observation of how they and their families spent their time, a household survey of new developments and a youth engagement exercise.

Figure 7.2 Northern Ireland street markings (Derry)
Source: extramuralactivity.com.

The data resulted in a graphic report that sketched out how the urban environment impacted on individuals on a daily basis, and informed design decisions. A short and inexpensive research phase conducted by two people offered the potential to create powerful social impacts. This strategy is useful for single site developments where an in-depth knowledge of the surrounding social or cultural landscape is required (Figure 7.2).

A dedicated Social Sustainability Assessment Framework: southern England, UK

The public can be consulted and social objectives aligned with desired social impact by using a dedicated assessment framework. This can be scaled up through replication on other comparable developments. In 2012, social scientists created a *Social Sustainability Framework* for UK housebuilder, The Berkeley Group, to measure the level of social sustainability in their 'housing communities' Woodcraft (2012), and meet their other objectives of 'improving residents' quality of life, well-being'. It was piloted on four developments in London and Hampshire, and is now applied to all their schemes.[6]

Thirteen indicators were created to measure three key dimensions: 'Social and Cultural Life', 'Voice and Influence' and 'Amenities and Infrastructure'. They are shown in the pie chart in Figure 7.3.

There is significant overlap between these indicators and key dimensions of social capital, cohesion, social sustainability and community resilience, and the various broad urbanist approaches mentioned in Chapter 4 as shown in Table 7.2. A similar framework could be created to measure a community's resilience.

The indicators were informed by questions from national data sets, industry standards assessment frameworks, and original questions that were locally relevant in the four developments. Residents at each site, 593 in total, were asked these questions in face-to-face interviews, and design professionals delivered a site survey for the 'Amenities and

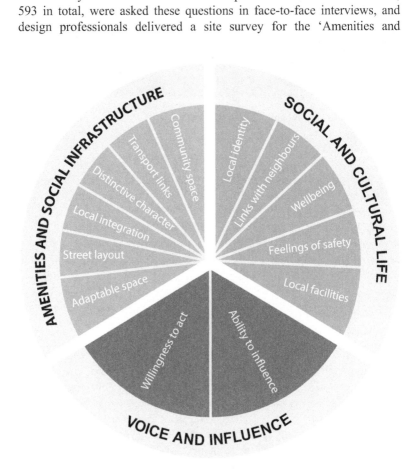

Figure 7.3 The Berkeley Group's indicators of social sustainability

Table 7.2 Overlap between Berkeley Group's indicators and social science/urban development concepts

Indicator	Social science or urban development concept that the indicator relates to
	Social and cultural life
Local identity	Social cohesion; desirable outcome of social capital
Links with neighbours	Social sustainability; community resilience
Well-being	Desirable outcome of social capital, social cohesion, social sustainability, community resilience
Feelings of safety	Social sustainability
Local facilities	Community resilience
	Voice and influence
Ability to influence	Desirable outcome of social capital
Willingness to act	Social sustainability; community resilience
	Amenities and infrastructure
Adaptable space	Research on uses of urban space post-disaster
Street layout	Principles of New Urbanism; TOD
Local integration	Principles of New Urbanism; TOD
Distinctive character	Principles of New Urbanism; TOD
Transport links	Principles of TOD
Community links	Principles of New Urbanism; TOD; Gehl on quality public spaces

Infrastructure' dimension. Contextual interviews with key property management, community and local government stakeholders aided the interpretation of data. The site survey was benchmarked against industry standards and the residents' survey against national datasets for comparable places within the UK. Responses to each indicator were ranked and colour-coded: Positive (Red), Satisfactory (Yellow) and Negative (Green) to make the results easy to interpret. The developer could check that they were meeting their objectives through the ranking of each indicator. Although the pilots were conducted retrospectively, the lessons learned are applied to all new schemes.

Community social resource or asset mapping

Community social resources in this context are social capital, cohesion and other related concepts such as social equity: intangible social process-based assets at work in the social environment. Social strengths are the specific dimensions of these concepts that are locally strong, for example, open networks, collective decision making, and sense of community. A community has 'needs' that may be absent strengths, e.g. more cohesive relationships, or ineffective dimensions, or 'weaknesses', such as tense relationships. More importantly, communities, even poor ones, have social resources and strengths that can be analysed using social resource or asset-mapping techniques, and built or bolstered up. Needs and weaknesses that need addressing can be identified using the same method.

These methods have origins in a concept and strategy called asset-based community development (ABCD), which is underpinned by social capital and social cohesion. ABCD aims to organise and empower communities to identify the tangible and intangible resources or 'assets' (Brown, Learmonth and Mackereth, 2015: 126) they can access or negotiate access to (Laverack, 2001: 140), and mobilise to address collectively perceived 'problems or goals' (Laverack, 2001: 139; Nutbeam and Harris, 2004: 31), and 'develop and implement strategies' (Nutbeam and Harris, 2004: 31) and actions to combat them. It is a core method in public health promotion programmes, those aimed at improving communities' social well-being, and others where communities are placed at the centre of their own destiny and influence outcomes. Its objectives centre around building communities' capacities (Nutbeam and Harris, 2004: 33) and empowering participants, especially vulnerable groups, through the act of participation (Brown *et al.*, 2015: 104). In practice, in ABCD, communities are usually linked with the staff of external organisations (Laverack, 2001: 140; Nutbeam and Harris, 2004: 32) to plan and implement interventions within the group social context over a long time frame. Through developing a sense of ownership over projects, becoming more aware of issues and devising solutions (Laverack, 2001: 139–140), learning new skills (Nutbeam and Harris, 2004: 32), and experiencing empowerment through gaining a sense of control and achievement of outcomes, communities improve their social and emotional health and well-being, and increase their capacity to address future situations. This model is an important tool in the development of social sustainability and the adaptive capacity to respond resiliently to crises.

When employed within urban development, a simple approach is participatory workshops where residents are prompted to identify and write down assets on sticky notes pinned to a board, as guided by maps or other area prompts. ABCD focuses on what works rather than deficits, and what could be even better in future. There are various methods for acquiring and strategising these two streams of information (see, for example, Emery, Fey and Flora, 2006). A more structured approach is found in the World Bank's Social Capital Assessment Tool (SCAT) (Krishan and Shrader, 1999) which uses different data collection methods to measure a community's social capital resources. These include structured group interviews, and household interviews that explore indicators of cognitive and structural social capital.

Another incarnation of ABCD was adopted by an NGO called *Catalytic Communities*, whose mission is highlighting and building on the existing social assets in Rio de Janeiro's *favelas*.[7] These informal residential settlements first emerged in 1897 and have grown and spread ever since. Due to a culture of *informality*, some *favela* residents respond creatively and imaginatively to the struggles of poverty and residential life, for example getting together to build a Christmas tree with neighbours on the main street, working together to build a day care centre, and responding as needed to improve social life without efforts being hampered by formal rules.

The NGO has observed important lessons for urban resilience born from the unregulated character of *favela* life as these neighbourhoods have mostly remained outside the Brazilian city's formal system. The importance of these assets even filtered into Rio's 1992 master plan recommendation to 'preserve their local character'. *Catalytic Communities* believes that formal urban communities around the world could benefit from such lessons, and not only cities in low- and middle-income countries.

In comparison with the formal city, Rio's favelas often exhibit greater:

- cultural production;
- sociability;
- atmosphere of play;
- strong undeniable sense of community;
- culture of collective action, or *mutirão*;
- intricacy in solidarity networks;
- use and early adoption of social media;
- adaptivity and talent for improvisation.

Physical features often lend themselves to community sociability:

- affordable housing in central areas, providing residences close to workplaces;
- low-rise, high density, mixed-use neighbourhoods;

- flexible and need-based architecture;
- narrow streetscape favouring pedestrians and engendering safe leisure spaces.

Co-design: Cape Town, South Africa

Co-design is the most democratic approach to uncovering a community's social needs from a physical development, their existing social resources and strengths, and devising design solutions. Design practitioners, government officials, civil society representatives and neighbourhood organisations work cooperatively with communities to identify and meet their needs, involving them in design, and/or construction. Co-design projects are an effective way of building social capital and strengthening collective capacity (essential for *adaptive capacity* and resilience), by drawing in networks of neighbours or co-residents. Communities can benefit from improved well-being and economic development in the longer term.

Cape Town's VPUU programme contains co-design methodologies. The programme includes extensive community involvement in the planning, implementation and management of urban renovations intended to design out crime. It helps the community to develop a sense of pride and ownership over their neighbourhoods. A feeling of ownership increases the likelihood that a person will invest time in their neighbourhood, and take care of it. It encourages them to attend to damaged infrastructure and boost their community's resilience after an environmental adversity.

The programme has a unique, multi-step methodology for fostering collaboration. A Baseline Survey[8] is carried out via a participatory Rapid Urban Appraisal methodology where the community participate in focus groups. The survey analyses violence and crime-related problems, community needs, potentials, and people's social organisational patterns in 'Safe Nodes', land spaces designated for treatment. Interactive, participatory workshops and public meetings, and the election of individuals to Reference Groups with professional stakeholders, draw the community into the planning, design, and implementation stages of VPUU. Local needs are thus addressed through dialogic mechanisms.

Conducting psychological and social research alongside co-design: Portland (Oregon), USA and Manchester, England, UK

Social and psychological scientists can participate in an urban programme, using sociological and psychological concepts to frame and evaluate

Figure 7.4 Stalls beside Khayelitsha Metrorail station, Cape Town
Source: http://bit.ly/2jcl20S.

whether community needs are met, and acquire the strongest evidence of the impacts of participation. They can measure social resources before and after a scheme's completion, and also monitor and evaluate inputs and impacts. Two projects with comparative methodologies, underpinned by psychological assessments, were run in Portland, Oregon, USA in 2003 (Semenza, March and Bontempo, 2006) and Manchester, UK, in 2011-2012 (Anderson, Ruggeri, Steemers and Huppert, 2016). Residents of three Portland neighbourhoods were recruited to restore three public squares in areas where residents lacked a sense of community and of place. The social objectives were improving their social capital and mental well-being. An existing social strength was willingness to participate.

A programme of steps was followed: 1) the community members were involved in group activities to analyse existing levels of social capital, and build upon it; 2) collaborative workshops were held with design professionals to build bridging social capital, and produce designs; 3) City Repair, a local NGO, facilitated stakeholder cooperation and programme implementation; 4) stakeholders helped the community to construct their designs; 5) psychologists helped community members input into the design of a survey tool to evaluate their mental well-being, social capital and community capacity (*adaptive capacity*) before and after the project. Students surveyed 265 residents all living in a two-block radius of each site, taking just under a month before the development, and 6 weeks afterwards.

The newly renovated squares were reported as being more attractive by researchers. They featured improvements such as a mural, interactive art, trellises, planters, and ecological installations including a lawn chessboard, cob benches and a light clay sauna. The researchers concluded that through community empowerment, participation and collective action, survey findings showed improvements in mental well-being, sense of community, community capacity, and an overall increase in social capital (Figure 7.5).

In Manchester, UK, community members recruited from forums and a Manchester City Council local resident database attended workshops where they were asked by urban designers to evaluate the shortcomings of parks and squares. Once more, an existing strength was willingness to participate. These volunteers proposed improvements to a small public space, sheltered by buildings, which they subsequently laboured to implement themselves. These included public art, free high-speed WiFi service, shade-tolerant planting, an inner-city lawn vegetation management, recycled seating, painting and general cleaning.

Before the regeneration, researchers identified three behaviours known to promote subjective well-being and physical health from a list of the five most important.[9] One of these is 'connecting with other people, whether familiar or strangers (e.g. talking and listening)'. To study whether the regenerated space encouraged more social connections than before refurb-

Figure 7.5 Portland neighbourhood squares
Source: Jan Semenza.

ishment, a researcher observed people's behaviour when using it,[10] and a similar, untouched space, both before and after the treatment. Observations were carried out on 22,956 people, over two 3-week periods during two consecutive summers, and coded in real time using a predefined checklist. The researcher sat on the edge of the space like a regular user, and recorded data into a digital tablet as if writing emails or surfing the internet. People connected near the outdoor exhibition space, picnic benches, walls, railings, bicycle racks and public art, thus demonstrating the behavioural influence of specific urban design characteristics.

Following the design intervention, there was a 394 per cent increase in the number of people who used the treatment space to 'connect', and no significant increase in the non-treated space during the same period. This cost-effective intervention empowered the volunteers by giving them decision-making powers, and enhanced their collective capacity (*adaptive capacity*), and also social connections among public space users. Forming social connections occurs through friendly interactions, a key dimension of our analytical frameworks (Figure 7.6).

Stage 3: design decisions and implementation

Design decisions: Belfast, Northern Ireland, UK, and Christchurch, New Zealand

Design choices for the characteristics of buildings or public spaces – their placement, layout, form and aesthetics – should be underpinned by information gathered at Stage 2 on local social and cultural context, a community's dynamics, resources, strengths and social needs (weaknesses). Two examples show this progression from the Research and Community Participation stage to Design Decisions.[11]

Case study 1: Belfast, Northern Ireland, UK

The anthropologists who mapped the cultural meanings of city spaces in Belfast produced ethnographic data showing how the direction of approach to a building could reveal sectarian identity as Protestant or Catholic. This was because walking routes passed in and out of or through claimed territory. In a city where tensions can quickly spark, people sometimes avoided routes that unmasked their affiliations for fear of retribution and violence. The researchers recommended locating the entrances of the planned complex in neutral space to avoid this problem. Design decisions have social and cultural implications that all developers should acknowledge, and thus take action to make sensitive choices.

(a)

(b)

Figure 7.6 Manchester participatory urban design intervention
Source: Jamie Anderson.

Case study 2: Christchurch, New Zealand

Marginalised people must have a voice in the community participation process, as in Health Impact Assessments (HIA) in New Zealand. Before the terrible earthquakes of 2010 and 2011, Christchurch City Council decided to expand and upgrade the city's Bus Xchange. An HIA[12] was carried out by public health professionals at scheme conception stage. Māori people, indigenous New Zealanders, shared their ideas on its design at several monthly community consultations called *Hui* (social assembly or gathering) with a view to creating positive social and health impacts. They proposed indigenous designs, native plants and a water feature to promote spiritual well-being. Recommendations also included seating to catalyse social interaction, and public activity space for artists and musicians. Their main stipulation was that the project was respectful of the Canterbury region's Māori (*Waitaha*) heritage. This marginalised segment of the population successfully brought fresh, culturally located design ideas to the plans.

Projected impacts of these features would be the social and health impacts of pleasant aesthetics and natural features; local residents'/users' positive regard for the place (a *component of a sense of place*); increased attachment to the improved urban environment; and a potential increase in the community's sense of responsibility for their urban surroundings.

Design decisions can have positive social impacts, such as supporting social cohesion. Community participation in design can give marginalised people, as well as the community in its entirety, a voice.

Implementation: Portland (Oregon) USA, Manchester, England, UK, and Cape Town, South Africa

Communities also benefit from having a role in implementing projects, as in our examples from Portland and Manchester. These communities increased their social resources. Volunteering in the renovation of public spaces can inspire attachments to the area and community or other psychosocial connections. In these two cases, it strengthened collective decision making and capacity to act, thus empowering people both individually and collectively. It increased the number of social connections made in public spaces, and improved participants' well-being.

Projects such as Cape Town's VPUU programme, which marry beneficial social objectives with actions that can be taken by community participants to strengthen their social resources and create economic and other opportunities, serve the dual purpose of achieving social development and producing a superior built environment. One of six design features implemented in the Khayelitsha neighbourhood of Harare was safer pedestrian passageways with paved walkways and street lighting. These provided 'safe routes' linking major entry and exit points through dense informal settlements. Well-lit spaces for gathering and informal trading were located alongside the main pedestrian routes. At the intersections were 'Active Boxes', small two- or three-storey buildings containing a meeting room, caretaker's flat and a room for facility guardians.

These were occupied round the clock providing surveillance. Hundreds of local volunteers were trained to operate unarmed neighbourhood patrols to deter crime under the Neighbourhood Watch Project. Safety on the streets has improved, feelings of safety being a psychological dimension of social sustainability. The scheme's overall success was directly quantifiable. The overall crime rate dropped by 20 per cent, and the murder rate by 39 per cent. This was the highest drop in a low-income community in the whole of Cape Town (James, 2012).

In another of the scheme's initiatives, women attended trauma counselling and bonded so closely that the whole neighbourhood went on to design positive public art to heal trauma, and convey pride in VPUU-funded amenities. Public amenities built included a football pitch, playground, youth centre and stalls for traders near the metro. A waste dump, formerly the scene of many murders, was turned into a park reported to be 'beautiful' and 'safe'. Many residents were employed in the management of amenities, and participated in the scheme's monitoring and evaluation process.

The VPUU has strengthened collective capacity, social cohesion and bonds – emotional connections that can underpin a sense of community among residents who can contribute to reducing crime and improving safety, thus increasing their well-being, and acquiring economic (trading) and employment opportunities.

Stage 4: monitoring and evaluation

Portland (Oregon), USA, Manchester, England, UK, and Yala, Thailand

A study strand within a project – as in Portland and Manchester – can allow a researcher to observe social inputs and evaluate whether defined social objectives are being met during implementation, building, and on completion. In both projects, researchers identified a social objective and a desired social impact. For example, in Portland: (*social objective*) encouraging collective action leading to (*social impact*) improved social capital and mental well-being. The study methodology of both projects encompassed data collection before and after the urban interventions to assess levels of social capital, which meant the successful assessment of the scheme's immediate impacts.

Ongoing monitoring must be an integral part of ensuring that plans are acted upon so that social objectives are operationalised. Post-completion evaluation is crucial for understanding social impacts and better informing future plans. The rationale behind social and health impact assessments (SIAs and HIAs), which are sometimes carried out on built environment developments, is useful. Both aim to anticipate the social and health impacts on communities in advance. Positive impacts can then be intentionally maximised.

Although often prospective, HIAs can be conducted before, during or after a development. In 2004 in the city of Yala in Thailand, the Ministry of Health conducted an HIA to assess the health and social impacts of the initial phase of The Garden City Project (Department of Health, Thailand, 2004), a scheme to build parks, gardens and green spaces for public benefit. Street vendors and residents were observed and interviewed in the new green areas. Researchers found increased socialisation with friends and newcomers and greater opportunities for income generation, informing a set of recommendations to further improve the project and residents' lives (Figure 7.7).

Figure 7.7 Yala Garden City HIA Project
Source: HIA Division, Department of Health, Thailand.

Given the various pressures faced by many projects – political, financial and budgetary, and time constraints – the social aspects of urban development can become a low priority during the implementation phase. Social observers, with the support of a project's backers, can be well placed to carry out ongoing monitoring during implementation and building, and post-completion evaluation. They can remind planning and design teams to honour their commitment to meet development objectives concerning social sustainability.

Three of the projects examined in this book had effective monitoring and evaluation methodologies. Each offers different benefits.

Robust data blending subjective and objective views: Delhi, India

The Indian team who explored the relationship between public open space and social interaction and neighbourhood relations in Delhi in Chapter 6 used a robust methodology. It blended qualitative with quantitative methods to amalgamate subjective (residents') and objective (observers') perspectives on the social impacts of these spaces. The urban layout was analysed from an expert urban planning point of view to isolate the aspects that may influence behaviours and psychological responses. An observational study was conducted to record who used the spaces, when and for what purposes.

Finally, 300 residents were interviewed for their opinions on the open spaces and affected behaviours. This approach could be usefully applied as an evaluation tool where renovation of an existing development is planned. Its strength is the combination of data conveying subjective views of how the spaces are experienced, and objective views recording overall trends in usage, raising the precision of the exact impacts identified.

Community empowerment: Cape Town, South Africa

In Cape Town's VPUU, social impacts are monitored and evaluated by residents, who collectively conduct a weekly Household Survey to look at results. This has revealed feelings of pride and safety in the new and renovated public spaces, which are well lit and vibrant. A monthly planning meeting between professionals and the community examines strategic decision making, endorsement of new plans, and performance evaluation. In the neighbourhood of Harare, these meetings regularly attract 120 people. 'Having a say' helps them trust the authorities and projects, and builds their sense of co-ownership. This increases the likelihood of care of their neighbourhood during calm periods and crises alike. Such initiatives draw residents into the heart of the scheme, affording feelings of investment, inspiration and empowerment, and building collective capacity. These methods are productive in participatory or co-design and development projects where the community is treated as a key partner in the mix of stakeholders.

Longitudinal monitoring and evaluation: southern England, UK

In 2014, the UK's Berkeley Group converted its *Social Sustainability Framework* into a toolkit (Berkeley Group, 2014) to encourage other developers and local government planners to apply the Group's social sustainability principles to new housing developments. The toolkit encouraged developers to consider how prospective tenants or residents, local stakeholders and others would respond to the 13 criteria in the original assessment framework at different stages of the development. In addition, it suggested good practice examples that developers could take – in the fields of pre-development research steps, and parameters for design, location and choice of facilities – to operationalise the 13 criteria. These could be factored into a plan to positively influence community behaviours and psychological responses. If we take Criterion 2: Links with Neighbours, it was matched with the following recommended actions:

Links with neighbours[13]

- This is about creating a place where people know their neighbours and trust each other.
- If you can encourage social interaction and social networks locally, this is strongly linked with lower crime rates and higher life satisfaction.
- Start by asking what would help people get on here: what would prompt people to stop and talk to their neighbours? Could you borrow things or ask for help?
- Design streets and squares so that they can be used as social and play spaces, not just a thoroughfare; think about the design and use of street furniture and benches, for example.
- Invest in neighbourhood projects that both new and existing residents will use, such as a sports or social club, or a way for people to connect online.

The toolkit could be applied before, during and up to two years after a development as a method of evaluating its long-term impacts. Table 7.3 illustrates when and why the toolkit should be applied and the methods used.

Table 7.3 Applying Berkeley Group's toolkit

Project stage	When and why apply it?	Methodology
Pre-development	During the design process as part of a planning application; alongside an Environmental Impact Assessment (EIA) as part of community engagement strategy	• Workshops test plans against the 13 criteria • Tweaking the plan to include prioritised criteria
Mid-stage	Any time after first phase is complete – allows the developer to see how early tenants feel, how design and governance could evolve, and how it compares to data on similar housing communities	• Site survey delivered by design professional • Comparative analysis using social data • Contextual stakeholder interviews • A final report
After completion	An evaluation 18 months to 2 years after residents have moved in – their lived experiences can be compared to similar places; data is supplied on performance of new community	• Site survey delivered by design professional • Comparative analysis using social data • Contextual stakeholder interviews • A final report

Adapted from Berkeley Group (2014: 18–19)

Finally, Berkeley offered the benefits of the toolkit:

> - For planners, these criteria will help you make informed judgements about the quality of applications and what is required from new housing to create a strong community.
> - It will help you convince the community and councillors (*local government officials*) that new proposals will genuinely add value to the local area and coherently address all the issues that affect people's quality of life.
> - Above all, it will help create places we are all proud of and where people want to live.
>
> Berkeley Group (2014: 2)

This approach is beneficial for the long-term monitoring and evaluation of schemes, and for application to multiple sites. The Berkeley Group used this kit on all its schemes, having committed to undertaking a formal assessment of pre-planning on all developments of more than 100 homes. This toolkit has some parallels with the rationale for a social impact assessment (SIA), although SIAs scope for a wider range of potential impacts (Figure 7.8).

Figure 7.8 Imperial Wharf, London
Source: Berkeley Group.

Behavioural and psychological effects or responses to projects

Our international examples have illustrated different approaches, tools and methods within four stages of a socially planned urban development process that urban development teams can adopt, and their influence on pro-community outcomes. Table 7.4 itemises the pro-community behavioural and psychological responses that we identified within the available data from each project, and the overall actual or projected[14] social impacts of these pro-community outcomes and the project itself.

Table 7.5 compares the dimensions in the 'socially sustainable community framework' with the actual pro-community behaviours that arose from the projects reviewed. In many cases, specific local variants on these dimensions were observed, fitting under the same broader conceptual category. This table is based on available data and scholarly projection.[15]

Five other categories of responses that indicate additional behavioural and psychological dimensions of social sustainability were identified. These are categorised in Table 7.6.

The built environment and socially planned urban development has a proven capacity to influence pro-community behaviours that are dimensions or outcomes of, or are closely related to social capital and social cohesion.

Table 7.4 Pro-community outcomes from projects reviewed for social sustainability

Project	Pro-community behavioural and psychological responses (projected or actual)	Overall social and well-being impact of pro-community behaviours and project itself (projected or actual)
Public Open Space, Delhi, India	*Actual outcomes:* *Behaviour:* • Visibility of social groups • Mixing of social groups • Increased social interaction • Increased social connection and social networks • Participation in community activities *Psychological:* • Pride in neighbourhood • Sense of community • Place attachment • Feelings of safety • Satisfaction with neighbourhood	*Actual outcomes:* • Improved urban environment • Increased social capital – particularly bridging social capital • Social integration/inclusion • Increased well-being

(*Continued*)

Table 7.4 (Cont.)

Project	Pro-community behavioural and psychological responses (projected or actual)	Overall social and well-being impact of pro-community behaviours and project itself (projected or actual)
VPUU, Cape Town, South Africa	**Actual outcomes:** *Behaviour:* • Volunteering and participation in civic activities • Collective action *Psychological:* • Sense of pride and ownership • Community bonds • Feelings of safety • Awareness of community needs *Social process with behavioural and psychological dimensions* • Improved social cohesion	**Actual outcomes:** • Improved urban environment and better living conditions • Increased social capital • Lower crime rates • Safer urban environment • Increased employment opportunities • Civic empowerment

(Continued)

Central Railway Station, Cape Town, South Africa	*Projected outcomes:* *Behaviour:* • Visibility of poor people in city centre public realm • Social mixing • Incidental social contact	*Projected outcomes:* • Improved urban environment • Increased trading opportunities for the poor • Increased bridging social capital • Social cohesion
Mixed housing complex, Belfast, Northern Ireland, UK	*Not applicable as no community follow-up*	*Intended impacts:* • Increased social cohesion • Improved feelings of safety
Social Sustainability Framework, UK	*Actual outcomes: headline findings from the four pilot tests* *Behaviour:* • Social contact with neighbours • Long-term residence (*plan to stay in the community*) *Psychological:* • Sense of belonging • Feelings of safety (*at 3 out of 4 developments*)	*Projected outcomes:* • More socially sustainable housing • Increased social capital • Improved feelings of safety • Increased well-being

(Continued)

Table 7.4 (Cont.)

Project	Pro-community behavioural and psychological responses (projected or actual)	Overall social and well-being impact of pro-community behaviours and project itself (projected or actual)
	• Feelings of happiness and levels of well-being	
Public Squares, Portland, Oregon, USA	***Actual outcomes:*** *Behaviour:* • Community participation • Collective action *Psychological:* • Place attachment • Sense of community • Empowerment	***Actual outcomes:*** • Improved urban environment • Increased collective capacity • Increased social capital • Increased mental well-being
Public space, Manchester, UK	***Actual outcomes:*** *Behaviour:* • Community participation in civic activities • Collective action	***Actual outcomes:*** • Improved urban environment • Increased collective capacity • Increased social capital • Increased mental and physical well-being

(Continued)

Bus Xchange, Christchurch, New Zealand

- Collective decision making
- Social interaction and connections

Projected outcomes:

Behaviour:

- Social contact
- Artistic activity

Psychological:

- Sense of pleasure and calm
- Sense of place
- Place attachment
- Sense of responsibility for urban surroundings

- Increased community empowerment

Projected outcomes:

- Improved transport hub
- Increased social capital
- Increased mental well-being

NB: Projected outcomes are based on CB's professional knowledge of HIAs and SIAs.

Table 7.5 Dimensions of a socially sustainable community compared with dimensions analysed in projects

Dimensions of a socially sustainable community	Behaviours and psychological responses identified in responses to the built environment and participation in development projects
Pride in and attachment to neighbourhood	• Pride in urban environment • Sense of community • Sense of place • Place attachment • Sense of belonging
Social interaction within the neighbourhood	• Incidental social contact • Social interaction and connections • Social contact with neighbours
Safety/security (versus risk of crime, antisocial behaviour)	• Feelings of safety
Perceived quality of local environment	• No exact data but implied in several projects (e.g. Delhi, Portland, VPUU)
Satisfaction with the home	• Satisfaction with the neighbourhood
Stability (versus residential turnover)	• Long-term residence (plan to stay in the community)
Participation in collective group/civic activities.	• Volunteering • Participation in civic and community activities and community affairs • Collective action • Artistic activity – if undertaken by community members

Table 7.6 Additional dimensions of social sustainability

Additional dimensions of social sustainability	Behavioural and psychological components of new dimensions
Happiness and well-being	• Sense of pleasure and calm • Feelings of happiness • Levels of well-being
Social connection	• Community bonds
Social cohesion, integration and inclusion	• Visibility of social groups • Mixing of social groups • Good levels of social cohesion • Awareness of community needs

(Continued)

Table 7.6 (Cont.)

Additional dimensions of social sustainability	Behavioural and psychological components of new dimensions
Social solidarity and community spirit	• Sense of ownership of urban environment • Sense of responsibility for urban surroundings
Voice, influence and civic empowerment	• Collective decision making • Empowerment

Notes

1 These case studies did not provide the data to analyse medium or longer-term social outcomes.

2 For further details on more traditional approaches, see the annotated bibliography in Kohlhepp (2012), which presents the typical stages as characterised in major real estate textbooks, and suggests a further detailing and characterisation.

3 This is not always the case with HIAs and SIAs, which have been known to start 'too late in the project planning process', Vanclay, Esteves, Aucamp and Franks (2015).

4 All VPUU material adapted from: VPUU website: www.vpuu.org.za/index2. php and OCED (unknown).

5 Residents of existing 'mixed' or 'neutral' areas may not share a community or social life with others from across the sectarian divide, rather simply just live alongside each other without violence.

6 Berkeley Group uses the toolkit on all schemes and has committed to undertake a formal assessment pre-planning on all developments of more than 100 homes. Source: Berkeley Group website.

7 All material of Rio de Janeiro's *favelas* taken from: Williamson (2017).

8 VPUU Website, 'Baseline Survey Short Description' at: www.vpuu.org.za/ _files/pages/Baseline_Survey_Short_description.pdf.

9 The five most important actions people can take to improve their well-being were derived from the evidence gathered in the Foresight Project on Mental Capital and Well-being, published by the UK Government's Office for Science in 2008. These five behaviours were identified in: Aked, Thompson, Marks and Cordon (2008).

10 A socio-demographic survey was also delivered in person prior to the intervention that recorded the profile of users at both spaces. Most users were from Manchester and North West England (Anderson *et al.*, 2016: 3).

11 These two case studies on Belfast housing and Christchurch's Bus Xchange, were unrealised plans due to 1) financial turmoil and 2) earthquakes. Both plans drew upon extensive social research with potential tenant and user

communities. CB used methods from ex ante HIAs and SIAs, to predict behavioural responses. The social data elicited from both involved communities included strong ideas for socially aware planning, also put forward by the anthropologists conducting social research with communities in the Belfast neighbourhoods around the planned housing complex.

12 All material adapted from: Ria (2009).
13 Source: www.berkeleygroup.co.uk/media/pdf/l/h/berkeley-social- sustainability-toolkit.pdf.
14 Woodcraft (lead researcher of the Berkeley Group Social Sustainability project) considered that although the pilot trials of the 'Social Sustainability Framework' resulted in pro-community behaviours, overriding outcomes were as yet 'projected' rather than 'actual'.
15 Projected outcomes are based on CB's professional knowledge and experience in HIAs and SIAs.

References

Aked, J, Thompson, S, Marks, N and Cordon, C (2008) *Five Ways to Well-being: The Evidence*, London: New Economics Foundation.

Anderson, J, Ruggeri, K, Steemers, K and Huppert, F (2016) 'Lively social space, well-being activity, and urban design', *Environment and Behaviour* 1–32. (online edition).

Berkeley Group (2014) *Creating Successful Places: A Toolkit*, accessed on 6 December 2015 at: www. berkeleygroup.co.uk/media/pdf/l/h/berkeley-social-sustainability-toolkit.pdf

Berkeley Group website (n.d.) accessed at: www.berkeleygroup.co.uk/sustainability/social-sustainability/creating-successful-place.

Brown, JS, Learmonth, AM and Mackereth, CJ (2015) *Promoting Public Mental Health and Well-Being: Principles into Practice*, London: Jessica Kingsley.

Cave, B (2015) 'Assessing the potential health effects of policies, plans, programmes and projects', in: Barton, H, Thompson, S, Burgess, S and Grant, M (eds), *The Routledge Handbook of Planning for Health and Well-being*, London: Routledge.

Department of Health, Ministry of Public Health (2004) *The Health Impact Assessment for Healthy Public Policy: A Case Study of 'Garden City Project' Yala City, Thailand*, accessed on January 2014 at: www.apho.org.uk/resource/item.aspx?RID=4767.

Emery, M, Fey, S and Flora, C (2006) 'Using Community Capitals to Develop Assets for Positive Community Change', *CDP Practice Issue 13*, accessed on 22 December 2015 at: http://srdc.msstate.edu/fop/levelthree/trainarc/socialcapital/communitycapitalstodevelopassets-emeryfeyflora2006.pdf

Fagence, M (1977) *Citizen Participation in Planning*. Oxford: Pergamon.

Fataar, R and Petzer, B (2014) 'Cape Town's anti-apartheid urban plan: Reclaiming a city from a history of hate', *Next City* website, 9 May 2014, accessed on 23 December 2015 at: http://nextcity.org/forefront/view/cape-towns-anti-apartheid-urban-plan

James, H (2012) 'How citizens and urban design beat crime', article for *Lee Kuan Yew World City Prize* website, accessed on 6 December 2015 at: www.leekua nyewworldcityprize.com.sg/features_khayelitsha.htm

King, S (1983) *Co-Design: A Process of Design Participation*, New York: Van Nostrand Reinhold.

Kohlhepp, D (2012) *The Real Estate Development Matrix*, paper presented at the American Real Estate Society Meetings, St Petersburg, Florida, April 21 2012, accessed on 6 December 2015 at: www.ccimef.org/pdf/2012-299.The-Real-Estate-Development-Matrix.4-21-12.pdf

Krishan, A and Shrader, E (1999) *World Bank Social Capital Assessment Tool*, prepared for the Conference on Social Capital and Poverty Reduction, The World Bank Washington, DC, June 22–24, 1999, accessed on 21 December 2015 at: http://siteresources.worldbank.org/INTSOCIALCAPITAL/Resources/Social-Capital-Assessment-Tool–SOCAT-/sciwp22.pdf

Laverack, G (2001) 'An identification and interpretation of the organizational aspects of community empowerment', *Community Development Journal* 36 (2): 134–145.

Nutbeam, E and Harris, E (2004) 'Chapter 3: Theories on change in communities and communal action for health', in: *Theory in a Nutshell* (2nd edn), Sydney: McGraw Hill, 10–24.

Pharoah, R, Norman, W and Hale, T (2007) *Sirocco Site: Community Consultation*. London: ESRO (Ethnographic Social Research).

Ria, A (2009) *Christchurch Transport Interchange: Health Impact Assessment* 2007/08 – 2008/09. Hui Facilitation and Maori Work Stream Report Writing. Report Prepared for Canterbury DHB.

Sanoff, H (2010) 'Democratic or participatory design: Introduction', in: *Democratic Design: Participation Case Studies in Urban and Small Town Environments*, Germany: VDM Verlag Dr Muller.

Semenza, JC, March, TL and Bontempo, BD (2006) 'Community-initiated urban development: an ecological intervention', *Journal of Urban Health: Bulletin of the New York Academy of Medicine* 84 (10): 8–20.

Vanclay, F (2002) 'Conceptualising social impacts', *Environmental Impact Assessment Review* 22: 183–211.

Vanclay, F, Esteves, AM, Aucamp, I and Franks, DM (2015) *Social impact assessment: guidance for assessing and managing the social impacts of projects*, Report for International Association of Impact Assessment, 98 pages, accessed on 6 December 2015 at: www.iaia.org/pdf/IAIA%202015%20Social%20Impact %20Assessment%20guidance%20document.pdf

Violence Prevention through Urban Upgrading website (n.d.) accessed at www.vpuu.org.za/index2.php and 'Baseline Survey Short Description', available at: www.vpuu.org.za/_files/pages/Baseline_Survey_Short_description.pdf

Williamson, T (2017) 'Rio's favelas: the power of informal urbanism', in *Perspectica* 50: Urban Divides. 213–228.

Woodcraft, S (2012) 'Social sustainability and new communities: Moving from concept to practice in the UK', *Procedia – Social and Behavioural Sciences* 68: 29–42.

8 Socially sustainable communities can also be resilient communities

Introduction

Chapter 8 highlights the importance of a socially planned built environment and public participation in urban development with maximum influence on community social resources for urban locations vulnerable to climate changed-related and other natural disasters. We offer six case studies located in five cities that show how relationships between the built environment/social infrastructure, and existing or lacking social organisational strategies grounded in pro-community behaviours hindered or promoted behavioural resilience during/after negative environmental events. The cases depict communities in developing and developed nations with both sufficient and insufficient socio-economic resources and urban infrastructure. We draw on the 'resilient neighbourhood community framework' to identify the social resources, and behaviours and psychological responses required for resilience.

Behaviours and psychological responses during environmental adversities

Case study: Poor social cohesion among flood-prone informal settlement dwellers in Surat, India

We show the impact of poor social cohesion on a poor community who live in a zone subject to flooding, based on the view conveyed in *Surat City Resilience Strategy* (SCRS).[1] Other references are indicated in chapter endnotes. Surat is a coastal port city in India situated on the banks of the Tapi River. Its Ukai Dam provides irrigation, power and flood defences, but its overflows and those from other tidal creeks running through the city cause periodic floods. Surat is expected to experience more extreme weather events and increased flooding as a result of climate change. Anticipated effects are rising temperatures, increased precipitation and rainfall, sea level rise, changing disease patterns, and increasing energy demand.[2]

Rural migrants from within the state of Gujarat (Saurashtra, its arid Northern reaches), and other states (especially Maharashtra, Uttar Pradesh and Orissa) comprised about 55 per cent of Surat's ever growing 4.5 million inhabitants in 2011. Migrants represent many cultures and ways of life, and speak different languages. They have lived in Surat for less than two decades and were drawn to the city at an unprecedented rate by its expanding industrial economy, and opportunities to work in, for example, textiles and diamond cutting and polishing. The poorest migrant workers lived in slums and informal settlements, owing to low incomes and a housing shortage, making up 80 per cent of all slum households. From 2001 to 2006 the number of slums grew from 307 to 406.

These settlements were situated on vacant lands, often along flood plains and on low-lying land, along tidal creeks, river banks or drainage lines (Govind and Verchick, 2015). Their dwellings were constantly at risk of flooding, and required evacuation during intermittent flood events. Surat Municipal Corporation (SMC) produced a 'vulnerability and capacity' index within the city's climate vulnerability assessment.[3] Low-income residents in settlements located closest to the river were found to be the most vulnerable to flooding, alongside middle and upper socio-economic groups residing on the first and second floors in peripheral areas.

Although overall community spirit is said to be strong in Surat, 'known for its strength to convert its adversity into advantage' (Achal and Padhya, 2014), regionally diverse slum inhabitants experienced a 'fragmented social landscape' (Asian Cities Climate Change Resilience Network, 2011: 20). City stakeholders[4] foresaw that it would worsen with time. The SCRS measured 'social capacity' within its capacity index in terms of networks and cohesion. These were found to be generally poor among slum and lower socio-economic groups, although stronger among Gujaratis working in the diamond industries. They were familiar with the regional way of life and closer to their home networks than textile workers from more distant states such as Orissa and Uttar Pradesh.

In 2011, it was observed that population growth and in-migration were changing the social dynamics with 'emerging social and cultural differences "reportedly" reducing social cohesion' (Asian Cities Climate Change Resilience Network, 2011: 34). This implied that there may have been strong bonding social capital among, but weak bridging capital between regional groups. Possible reasons among recent arrivals included newness of networks, unestablished positions in these, and differences hindering the development of cross-regional networks. Poor migrants with little job security often returned to their home towns or moved to other cities.[5] Although no lengths of residence in the city were given, short stays affected the stability and depth of networks. A health study also identified heterogeneity and poor social cohesion among migrants, who were 'male predominant, poorly literate, busy in non-skilled jobs, with a main goal of earning and survival and living under uncertainty' (Ghanekar *et al.*, 2014: 3). Meeting these needs and combating known problems, such as landlord exploitation, may have necessitated immediate cooperation with regional connections because of inherent loyalties and mutuality, limiting time to invest more widely.

Social fragmentation and lack of cohesion negatively affect building resilience (*lack of bridging social capital and social cohesion*). Also, rural migrants have low levels of education and skills (*human capital*) and a limited stake or time to be involved in the city's wider development, thus the SMC perceived awareness of flood risks and climate change among this population sector as difficult. The health study found that migrants viewed the city as a workplace, and 'hardly imagine contributing to the climate change and health resilience' (Ghanekar *et al.*, 2014: 3). This is not surprising given the realities of the labour and services markets, and highlights the magnitude of the challenge.

SMC also experienced challenges in housing the migrant population, which was growing faster than the city's capacity to accommodate it. Building on flood plains had to be avoided but there was a shortage of suitable housing. Since 2015, SMC has stopped giving permission to build here (Chatterjee, 2015). There was also a lack of information on services available in the informal settlements. Some dwellers were relocated, and 22,000 new permanent houses built for them, with more under construction. One problem was that when people were relocated to safer townships a few kilometres away from the urban heart and their livelihood opportunities, social networks, and access to city services, many simply moved back to the slums illegally, re-increasing their vulnerability to the adverse effects of floods (Govind and Verchick, 2015). Thus they were driven by short-term survival requirements, viewing resilience as a longer-term luxury. SMC recognised the importance of drawing the migrants and lower socio-economic groups into the conversation about planning for resilience, and advocated finding ways to increase their social capital and capacities to 'build resilience through better coordination and mutual support' (Asian Cities Climate Change Resilience Network, 2011: 38).

Case study: The impacts of gender in physical spaces and community resilience in Khulna, Bangladesh

Demographic factors such as gender, socio-economic status, ethnicity and race, religion, disability, sexuality and age can influence who is present in different physical places, what they do there, exposure to adverse weather, and opportunities for cultivating behavioural resilience. In all cities, psychological responses to spaces such as feelings of safety, security and sense of belonging can determine the people who populate and use them. In the Bangladeshi city of Khulna,[6] gender profoundly shapes the extent to which women and men from low-income households in informal settlements go about their domestic, income-generation and civic activities in private, semi-public and public spaces. Their presence in these spaces directly impacts their exposure, sensitivity, and abilities to cope with and adapt to hazardous weather.

Khulna, Bangladesh's third largest city, is located in a region that has experienced climate changes in terms of rising temperatures and humidity, stronger monsoons, and an increase in rainy days. The region experiences pluvial flooding and water-logging, salinity intrusion into rivers and ground water aquifers, frequent and intense cyclones and storm surges, fluvial flooding from merging rivers, and heat waves impacting water scarcity. We discuss physical spaces from two settlements through which the *Rupsha River* flows.

The first, *Rupshachor*, is densely populated with 207 households per acre. It was developed on public land near a flood embankment adjoining fish-processing factories that provided job opportunities for women. The second, *Railway colony and Greenland abashon*, takes a linear form along the river and houses various clusters. It now comprises an average of 54 households per acre, who have gradually moved in over the years. Homes perch on low-lying public land near the railway station, river port, goods storage and retail markets where residents can access work.

These residents are well aware of the main climate hazards: water-logging accompanied by high-tide and storm surges, extreme temperature variability, and drinking water scarcity and associated health risks during the dry season of March to May. Exposures to these are differentially distributed depending on the mix of spaces that women and men access. The territorialisation of the built environment according to the gender norms of who inhabits spaces impacts opportunities for social contact and the efficacy of collective civic action: essential social resources for community resilience. People's understanding of the gendered 'norms' of inhabiting each space, as underpinned by power relations between men and women, shapes their access to resources and decision-making powers to take action to reduce the impacts of climate hazards. We show this situation in three types of built spaces.

Private spaces: Many households reside in one-room houses due to economic conditions and a shortage of affordable space. Local patriarchal social and moral norms for women, and economic and spatial constraints, dictate that they routinely carry out domestic and household management tasks in the privacy of their home. Houses do not have proper ventilation, are constructed from heat-absorbing materials, and indoor cooking causes fumes. These features increase health risks from heat exposure and indoor air pollution, especially among women. Some houses are also more exposed to heavy rain and water-logging, making it difficult to carry out household tasks.

Most women interact with others when they go out to wash and fetch water from deep tube-wells or use common baths located along the narrow streets. Yet here they remain exposed to rain or direct heat from the sun. These interactions do, though, foster social networks, trust and a sense of community. Other opportunities for group socialising, network-building and maintenance occur in houses and adjacent courtyards. For full protection from weather hazards, purpose-built semi-public spaces are needed, planned and sometimes built by individual households, especially by women with community leadership roles. As part of housing designs, some of these spaces feature seating, shade and ventilation for relief from the heat. Dedicated places for socialising that integrate protective design features, mitigating detrimental effects, address two resilience issues in one: cultivating stronger social networks, and protecting health and well-being.

Parochial spaces: The term 'parochial spaces' (Loftland, 1989) has a similar meaning to the urban design term 'transitional spaces'. They are between the 'private' space of the household and the anonymity of the public realm, a spatial transition zone from one to the other. Because social and moral norms limit the spatial mobility of many women and girls in fully public spaces, intermediate parochial spaces offer them refuge from the daily limits. Many women run small businesses such as preparing food or street trading or vending in or near their houses, in narrow spaces within and around their settlements, or beside roads, railway tracks and playing fields. In denser *Rupshachor* these types of spaces are hard to find. They are more abundant in *Railway colony* and *Greenland abashon*, yet are unprotected from climate hazards. Here women suffer from direct sunlight and intense rain. The relegation of women to these incidental spaces leaves them exposed to destructive meteorological forces. For example, water-logging after extreme events can destroy and interfere with their business activities. However, home-

Figure 8.1 Parochial space, Khulna, Bangladesh
Source: Huraera Jabeen.

based isolation can negatively impact women's ability to forge bonding social capital with co-workers as the cornerstone of community resilience (Figure 8.1).

These effects are somewhat off-set when circumstances allow individuals to extend and simultaneously climate-proof their private space to conduct business beside the home. Rani, a mother of five, who ran a tea stall on her veranda, made her plinth water-resistant, reduced waterlogging, and erected corrugated iron sheets on the roof and around the enclosure as part of a larger extension of her premises. This development, made worthwhile when the ward commissioner assured secure tenancy from 2009, improved protection from rain and high wind. Consequently, with increased income, Rani joined an NGO-led savings group to acquire capital for further development, and found herself contributing to community planning to improve the adjacent streets. She was able to use her agency to concurrently expand her income, climate-proof her environment, and empower herself within the wider residential network by having a voice and influence on neighbourhood design (Figure 8.2).

Figure 8.2 Woman outside her home, Khulna, Bangladesh
Source: Huraera Jabeen.

Public spaces: Men and boys living in the settlements frequent the public spaces of their neighbourhoods, located along the main access roads and river. Here they work in labour-intensive jobs and socialise at tea-stalls along the road, mosque, labour-union, and offices of cooperatives and political parties. Labourers working in open air spaces face occasional difficult weather conditions, but are protected from rain and heat in the semi-open social spaces. An example of this is the use of waterproof plastic sheets hung from the tea stands that also provide shade. Social capital is forged here as the men interact and communicate, sharing information on work opportunities and strengthening social and professional networks. They also congregate in open spaces near the river for relief from the heat during the evenings and nights. Women use these spaces in a more ephemeral way, on their way to work and the shops, thus losing out on the climate relief and social network-strengthening, and behavioural resilience-building opportunities offered to men.

Female occupants participate in purposeful initiatives to build their social networks and economic capital, and gain civic empowerment in alternative physical places, especially in parochial spaces they help create. In both neighbourhoods, NGO activities involved women in, for example, female-dominated groups for improving infrastructure, socio-cultural activities and events. Some of these women maintain alliances with political parties and representatives of local government yet are not expected to sit in party offices or linger in other major public social spaces frequented by men. An exception is a vegetable market established by older women that facilitated time for them away from their homes. They could network with neighbours and converse with fellow interest group members, and simultaneously build social capital. A donor-funded development programme enabled savings-group members and market vendors to nominate physical improvements to the market place, giving them voice and influence (Figure 8.3).

Figure 8.3 Market space managed by women, Khulna, Bangladesh
Source: Huraera Jabeen.

Climate change is a force for adverse change affecting the whole of humanity. Yet the story of the spatial separation of Khulna's poor women and men particularly disadvantages women from gaining maximum protection from destructive weather elements. Gender inequality is a threat to resilience. More women than men live in cities globally (Chant and McIlwaine, 2016; cited in Jabeen, 2017: 2) yet they suffer from a higher degree of exposure and sensitivity to climate hazards, and lower adaptive capacity to make changes. Public spaces are a key site for the emergence of resilient behaviours and states of mind. They should be able to accommodate entire communities on ordinary days when social mixing takes place, and in extreme times, when they can be used in alternative ways, such as for meeting and sleeping.

Case study: Good social capital before and after an urban environmental disaster: Surat, India, and Jakarta, Indonesia

There can be a huge difference in response to environmental adversities between communities with good levels of social capital and cohesion and those without, such as Surat's impoverished migrants.[7] We discuss Surat's middle-classes, followed by the *kampung* dwellers of the city of Jakarta, Indonesia.

Surat, India

People who have lived in Surat for generations are colloquially known as 'Surtis' and represent culturally diverse backgrounds.[8] Social networks, cohesion and mutual support were found to be strong among most communities from Gujarat. 'Social capacity' was measured most highly among middle and upper socio-economic groups. People with sufficient income who were not struggling to meet their basic needs may have had more time to devote to wider community issues, and perhaps had more to gain from developing networks. Longer residence meant stronger social networks and more developed relationships. The Surtis' social resources resulted in a high level of civic commitment, and pro-community behaviours, especially among older residents, who felt strongly connected to the city. They participated in urban development as part of their routine life. Pride and a sense of belonging were said to be evident from the 'sacrifices' they had made in the interests of the community and improving its quality of life, such as bearing a higher cost for the delivery of better services. They supported the city's cleanliness, solid waste management and water supply schemes.[9]

Their social resources during periods of calm – especially cohesion and interest in the collective good – translated into resilient, pro-community behaviours of helping the community following crises. These have included a plague (1996), floods (2002, 2006) which in 2006 inundated 75 per cent of the city, and bomb attacks (2008). After such crises, civil society organisations collaborated with SMC and industrial organisations. Surtis made sacrifices: for example, people gave up land for road widening and decongestion after the plague. According to one blog, after the 2006 floods they acquired 40 mechanical diggers, and several hundred people cleared the streets themselves, operating the diggers 24 hours a day in teams. Life returned to normal in just three weeks (Flora, 2012). Surtis also accepted changes in the rule levels of Ukai Dam after these floods. They cooperated with the SMC in discussing issues, and looking at ways of reducing risks and vulnerabilities.

The Surtis behave in both socially sustainable and resilient ways, caring for their urban environment and community. Although fostering social cohesion is more of a challenge among a socio-demographically diverse population, it is possible, and can be an asset for urban development. However, it does require that city leaders in both private and public realms acknowledge the different challenges and time horizons faced by different groups, especially poorer migrants.

Analysis

- The participation of diverse people, who represent a variety of perspectives and interests in urban planning, can identify a greater range of needs, possible inputs, impacts and longer-term outcomes.
- Cities that cater to a wider variety of perspectives and interests may attract wider investment.
- Diverse perspectives, interests, skills and values can mean more resources and strengths to draw upon during adversities, as our forthcoming New Zealand case shows. Such diversity, however, can also create additional challenges that must be addressed.

Jakarta, Indonesia

Some low-income people living in Jakarta, Indonesia's capital city, have strong social capital and social cohesion and cope effectively with environmental adversities. They live in the city's *kampungs* (informal settlements).[10] Their story tells how the informal physical environment partly shapes the pre-conditions for social capital.

Jarkarta is a harbour city with extensive low-lying areas susceptible to excessive flooding. The causes include heavy rainfall, high tides, and increased water run-off from voluminous groundwater tapping as part of redevelopment in upstream areas. Floods are set to increase due to greater urbanisation, and a natural astronomical cycle inducing sea level rise. The potential adverse effects of climate change are not even factored for.

Kampung residents are not always the poorest. *Kampungs* typically are settlements on state-owned or land not traded on formal markets so that inhabitants, who lack the legal land titles, can be evicted at any time. Densely populated, they contain low-quality housing: two-storey houses built close together and for the poorest, makeshift wooden houses on stilts in the river and river bed. Two *kampungs* in the neighbourhoods of Tomang and Manggarai are discussed. Both usually experience smaller floods during the rainy season and larger ones approximately every five years, such as a catastrophic flood in 2007.

Kampung residents are ethnically, culturally and religiously diverse, and comprise poor regional migrants and low-income formal sector workers and government-worker professionals. The slightly higher income inhabitants experience the advantages of close proximity to employment, healthcare and education, reduced transport and living costs, and time saved in the inner city *kampungs*.

The *kampungs'* spatial arrangements, and community and neighbourhood-level organisations, have contributed to good social capital and cohesion. Tomang's *kampung* is physically isolated from other residential areas. Manggarai's *kampung* overlaps with the administrative borders of the formal neighbourhood association. These boundaries reinforce people's sense of community. Houses in both are overbuilt and attached to each other, locating families and neighbours close together. People mingle on the small paths in front of their homes. Tomang's *kampung* lacks open spaces, so people meet on the path by the dam or at informal shops, restaurants and mobile carts. People can meet and talk in Manggarai *kampung*'s public spaces, coffee shops, and a small park (which can host public meetings). Intense social ties are built, particularly between neighbours, who exchange news and information.

Residents lack formal authority and municipal assistance, so their shared experience of socio-economic hardship and a continually insecure situation promotes a sense of community.[11] *Kampungs* are, however, integrated into the formal administrative system through the work of organisations known as RW/RTs, which also enhance the feeling of community. At neighbourhood level, *Rukun Tetangga* (RTs), and community level, *Rukun Warga* (RWs) organise and regulate the *kampung* communities. They run collective action schemes that manage the physical environment, maintain safety, and care for residents: for example, *kerja bakti* – a weekly communal activity to clean up the neighbourhood, whether the canal, garbage or public toilets, and *ronda* – a neighbourhood security system requiring voluntary participation. Residents often help neighbours meet costs for difficult events such as death and problems of old age. These organisations also connect them to various formal structures of government and support services (*vertical/linking social capital*).

Strong, trusted and effective voluntary leaders appointed from within the community, enforced integration of newcomer rural migrants, and sanctions against non-participants, such as exclusion from the neighbourhood or fees payable to a fund, ensure that social order and agency are successful. Consequently, inhabitants feel connected to each other, and develop cohesive relationships with neighbours.

Effective social capital and social cohesion have created communities that are self-organised, self-regulating and self-reliant (*adaptive capacity*). These strengths sustain residents during daily life, so they can then enact resilient pro-community behaviours when the floods come. Residents know what causes flooding. They view the floods as temporary and not disruptive of ordinary life, returning home once the water has drained away.

Analysis

Social capital-linked actions include:

- Friends and relatives in upstream areas text or phone, or municipal employees at flood gates communicate, to warn about floods several hours ahead. This compensates for an ineffective formal warning system.
- When warnings are received, residents move their valuables to the second floor of their homes. This strategy results from experience and resilience.
- The RW system evacuates people trapped in their homes and coordinates relief activities, kitchens and supplies.
- It helps the community pool its resources so that all have adequate food and water.
- People have a security system to prevent looting.
- Trusted community leaders coordinate the community's flood management activities. They also help organise coping activities that promote the collective interest and present a united front.
- *Kerja bakti* is operationalised in Manggarai to clean up homes and the neighbourhood.
- The RW also utilises networks established with external organisations.

Poverty does not preclude a community from developing good social capital and cohesion. Hardship can force the development of social resources and improve adaptive capacity. However, this is not a solution in itself. A city government must adequately house its citizens, rather than leaving a population who are 'surviving', in a permanent state of insecurity. Given their social resources, any subsequent effort to rehouse them must consider the following:

- Research must be conducted to understand the spatial and organisational features of a dwelling area that produce social networks and coping strategies among low-income people. These may help them generate a livelihood and produce the social ties and organisational forms needed to cope with hardship as a community.
- The outcome of relocating such communities is unpredictable. Sometimes socio-economic patterns and spatial proximity have produced circumstantial communities among heterogeneous people that may not otherwise have existed. Such communities may prove ephemeral when shared circumstances and location are removed. Alternatively, a known problem in Jakarta is that sometimes relocated communities are rehoused in accommodation that breaks down their networks and coping strategies. When they lack spatial and organisational opportunities to maintain these, and face socio-economic difficulties in the new location, they sometimes return to the original one to recapture these life supports.[12] Relocation plans must be preceded by in-depth research to anticipate the factors that may break up or keep communities together, and the support they need access to in new dwellings (Figure 8.4).

Case study: Recreating social capital in transitional housing after Hurricane Katrina on the Gulf Coast, USA

An American case illustrates the sensitive intertwinement between a city's physical structure and a community's social organisation, and the full force of social impacts when these are separated after an environmental adversity.

During routine life, urban form can influence positive social contact, behaviours and psychosocial attachments and other responses. Networks of neighbours (*structural social capital*) can support each other by taking actions (*collective capacity/efficacy*). Attachments to the local area and community can encourage people to take responsibility for, and care for others (*social support > desirable outcome of social capital*) and their urban infrastructure (*solidarity/community spirit as features of social cohesion*). When deadly weather events strike – such as Hurricane Katrina, which hit the Gulf Coast of the USA in Louisiana and

Figure 8.4 Kampung Manggarai, Jakarta
Source: Mario Wilhelm.

Mississippi on 29 August 2005 – housing can be destroyed. In Mississippi, one million people were displaced and $80 billion in property damage was caused. When people are displaced from their urban environment, social resources among neighbours can be negatively impacted with detrimental social and health impacts. Disaster and conflict exacerbate existing fractures along social lines, causing conflict and disruption on a community level (Erikson, 1978).

Residents of the city of New Orleans, Louisiana, many of whom had never left their neighbourhoods before, were given three forms of transitional housing.[13] Accommodation was underwritten by the Federal Emergency Management Agency (FEMA) or supported by private religious organisations (e.g. Lutheran Ministries) or NGOs. The accommodation strategy paid little regard to the preservation of communities' social resources. There was no understanding that these must be preserved by transferring networks of residents into temporary housing solutions that keep them intact. We explored how far this was successful in the three housing types.

Tent camps: People were not assigned by neighbourhood networks to these short-term options, but their layout supported some social resources. Community spaces were centrally located and tent entrances faced each other, supporting casual social contact and social monitoring, hence safety. Facilities such as showers were centrally located and services were nearby. Children had safe spaces for play. A degree of supportive community life was retained that enabled social capital and collective efficacy (*adaptive capacity*).

Cruise ships: Families of four living near ports, rather than neighbourhood groups, were accommodated on board. Each had two cabins and individual bathrooms. Meals, kitchens, educational and medical facilities, and medical staff plus state support agency representatives were available. Social spaces for gatherings and organised activities were provided which meant that neighbourhood acquaintances may have found each other, reducing the stress of displaced communities. However, families conflicted in the close proximity of the small spaces, requiring intervention by security personnel, resulting in high stress levels.

Trailers: Some families were lodged in cramped trailers on their collapsed home sites or in trailer parks as a transitional option. The spatial layout of their placement in such parks was detrimental to social capital and health. They were located far from town centres and tent camps. Trailer fronts, but not the windows, faced the street and stood between rows of other trailers. The door of one faced the side of another. There were no communal spaces or walkways due to lack of pre-planning and hurried construction. There was no social monitoring, poor security, and poor access to goods, services and transport. Elderly and vulnerable people suffered without access to community and health support, and many problems were recorded. People tried to leave these parks as quickly as possible.

The lack of human visibility and spatial opportunities to bond with others, and obtain social support, would have increased feelings of isolation and displacement, and negatively impacted on well-being. The cramped conditions increased the chances of conflict. The lack of social monitoring would have lessened feelings of safety and decreased social cohesion.

Social ties and community bonds (*cognitive social capital*) are important features of well-functioning communities, and can cushion the effects of natural disasters on physical and mental health and well-being. The stress of losing a home and a community after a disaster is twofold, and may exacerbate pre-existing vulnerabilities in individuals, increase the risk of negative social and health impacts, and impede recovery and resilience. The physical form of cities and human behaviour and psychological response are intertwined, particularly urban form's ability to support sustainable communities. Therefore, the housing and psychosocial needs of communities must be jointly addressed after a disaster.

The observational team of a psychologist, architect and mental health clinician, who analysed the social impacts of the temporary accommodation, made some recommendations for future disaster planning:

- Accommodation needs, the location of current residents, and social capital resources should be mapped as part of disaster preparedness and community resilience strategies.
- Collaborative urban design – with its community capacity building and empowerment qualities – using iterative design 'charettes' charting suitable temporary housing and rebuild plans – should be routine practice in disaster-prone zones. They can match the community's social and health needs with the physical form, and be implemented post-disaster (or if necessary, rapidly prepared) by a team of planners, social, psychological and health specialists.
- Temporary and transitional housing should be allocated so as to keep neighbours and cultural groups together.
- Social spaces must be provided amid post-disaster accommodation to promote social contact, bonds/shared experiences and support.
- Small cottages, made from hurricane-resistant materials, can be constructed and placed on former housing sites to maintain pre-existing social networks and social resources, or arranged in courtyards to promote social interaction and monitoring.
- 'Incremental housing' – where a core structure is constructed from readily available materials and additional rooms can be built as financial resources allow – can be built on existing sites to maintain social networks and social resources.

Case study: How socially sustainable communities are more resilient communities after earthquakes in Christchurch, New Zealand

We finally explore the impacts of the series of devastating earthquakes in the city of Christchurch, and region of Canterbury, New Zealand, on the built environment and four out of six communities surveyed locally. Major quakes occurred in September and December 2010, and February, June and December of 2011. They were unusually intense, creating colossal damage to urban and suburban communities. The February earthquake peak ground accelerations (which describe an earthquake's intensity) were among the highest ever recorded worldwide.

This story supplies a city-level overview of how resilient these different communities were, rather than examining just one population group or neighbourhood. It compares the urban infrastructure, social capital and cohesion before these horrific catastrophes – therefore their urban social sustainability – then immediately after, and up to 15–17 months afterwards. We see the difference that having socially planned community facilities and spaces, and strong relationships, networks, and organisational abilities before seismic destruction makes to communities in its aftermath, as compared to a lack of these.

We acknowledge that other factors affect resilience. Socio-economic hardship and deprivation weakened residents' ability to be resilient. However, groups experiencing low socio-economic status, ethnic diversity or minority or marginalised ethnicity still had strengths linked to pre-existing social cohesion. Pre-existing institutional support for poorer people and social cohesion are important precursors of community resilience. New Zealand is a Westernised nation with an indigenous population, the Māori people. Māori cultural values underpinned a highly effective earthquake response by *Ngai Tahu* (the largest tribe in the South Island), demonstrating that minority or marginalised people's worldviews can be rich resources for urban planning and disaster response strategies.

Research seeking to understand the factors assisting and restricting community resilience was conducted by a group of health organisations: Canterbury District Health Board (Community and Public Health), Mental Health Foundation, University of Otago, and Quigley and Watts Ltd (a consulting company).[14] The research comprised a literature review, document analysis and qualitative fieldwork undertaken from May to July of 2012, some 15–17 months after the earthquake of February 2011. The data are based on the perceptions of residents ('ordinary citizens') and community leaders interviewed 15–17 months after. Profiles of the four communities are given in Table 8.1.

We profile the built environment and community infrastructure, social capital and social cohesion, and community participation in urban planning in the four communities before, immediately after, and 15–17 months after the quakes.

Figure 8.5 185 Empty Chairs art installation representing lives lost, Christchurch
Source: Louise Thornley.

1) Built environment and community infrastructure

> Community infrastructure consists of venues and spaces for community
> life, and organisational structures that create social networks or link
> residents to networks and community leadership, and the support that
> these can engender.

Headline findings

- Physical venues and spaces – community halls, shops, libraries, parks, cafes, pubs – and walkable communities that provided incidental and organised social contact, contributed to strong social capital before the earthquakes. The loss of venues afterwards reduced social interaction, affecting social connections and resilience.
- The flexible use of buildings and spaces was crucial to setting up help centres and alternative venues for community meetings,

Table 8.1 Four Christchurch communities

Name of community	Profile	Impacts of earthquakes
Lyttelton	• Port town 12 miles from Christchurch – separated by hills • Population: 3000 • 84.8% NZ European + a prominent Māori community • Mixed occupational profile	• Buildings on main street destroyed e.g. historic churches • Supermarket, pubs, restaurants, meeting venues – unusable • 2 deaths • Residents left unsure if properties safe for rebuild for a long time due to potential rock fall
Shirley* *Research focused on a social housing neighbourhood	• Suburb 5km from centre • Population: 7000 • Above average ethnic diversity, e.g. Māori and Pacific Islanders • Low income • Many single or sole parent households • Public housing	• Damaged roads, land, property, power, water, wastewater • Liquefaction and dust • Transport problems, lack of shops and medical services • Displacement, disruption, hardship
Inner City East	• Near central business district • Population: about 3500	• Damaged land, property, power, water, wastewater • Silt from liquefaction

(Continued)

	• Deprived: low incomes, less home ownership • Affordable housing for low-incomes • Above average ethnic diversity, e.g. fewer NZ European, more Māori, Pacific and Asian residents	• 2 deaths and some injuries • Displacement of residents
Marae (Māori meeting houses/cultural community centres)	• Located in rural and urban areas, focus on *Rēhua marae* in suburb and 3 rural *marae* • Paid and volunteer leaders and workers • Community hubs for extended families (*whānau*), individuals with kinship, tribal or other links with kinship, tribal or other links • Accommodation for some residents • Facilitate celebration of Māori culture, the Māori language (*Te Reo Māori*) and tribal (*iwi*) obligations	• Minor damage at *Rēhua marae* and several rural *marae*; severe damage at one rural *marae* – to buildings, homes, meeting house, accommodation • Largest tribe (*iwi*) on NZ's south island – the *Ngāi Tahu* – used *Rēhua marae* as a hub for earthquake response for Māori and non-Māori in Christchurch • One rural *marae* provided support to the other *marae*

social events, and public performances when the usual facilities were damaged. Communities need physical focal points. Highlights of improvised uses of the built environment were:

- a parking lot used as a temporary public square for meetings, recreational events and festivities (Lyttelton)
- *Gap Filler* – a scheme where vacant sites were used to create temporary spaces for people to offer collective projects, e.g. colourful art and recycled park benches covering an old site (Inner City East)

- The loss of fondly regarded historic buildings – ordinarily fuelling attachments to place and collective community identities – had negative psychological effects. Creative uses of the denigrated built environment can provide some relief.
- Pre-existing, strong community-level organisations with links forged to residents before the earthquakes were already poised to support them afterwards, directly impacting resilience. Trusted leaders knew their communities' needs and acted accordingly. Communities without such robust structures fared worse afterwards (Figure 8.6 and Table 8.2).

2) Social capital and social cohesion

Good levels of social capital and cohesion in communities underpin their social sustainability. Related cultural concepts such as the Māori values of *manaakitanga* (caring and hospitality), *kotahitanga* (the *iwi* acting in one accord to support the people of Christchurch, regardless of race, culture or ethnic identification), *whanaungatanga* (a sense of family connection) and *korero* (the opportunity to talk) have a similar emphasis.

Headline findings

- Good social capital and cohesion in communities, or care-oriented cultural values, before the earthquakes directly impacted on the amount of community-level (not individual-level) support[15] that people provided afterwards. People in communities that lacked

Figure 8.6 Temporary social space, Christchurch
Source: Louise Thornley.

social capital (e.g. Shirley) beforehand were less proactive and resilient at community level afterwards.
- The following pre-existing social capital-linked factors influenced levels of resilient pro-community behaviours after the earthquake across all four communities:
  - Good communications with neighbours
  - Participation in community and civic events
  - Social solidarity/community spirit (awareness of the need to act for the good of the community)
  - Having shared values (e.g. the Māori) or social strengths that created pride, bonds, and attachments to place or community, e.g. a collective identity based on historic factors or good social cohesion amid ethnic diversity.

- Formal and informal community-level support improved the well-being of both givers and receivers through positive psychological

Table 8.2 Built environment and community infrastructure

Name of community	Before the earthquakes	Immediately after	In the medium term (up to 15–17 months after)
Lyttelton	Geographic isolation and small scale bounded the community	*Positives:*	*Positives:*
	• Geographic isolation and small scale bounded the community	• Community venues used as help centres	• Community organisations helped
	• Incidental social contact on main street	• Leaders and volunteers pro-active in helping community	• Spaces appropriated for community events when normal venues closed
	• 18 meeting venues	• Music festival hosted on street	
	• 28 community organisations with strong leadership		*Negatives:*
			• Loss of amenities reduced incidental social contact
			• Loss of historic buildings impacted collective community identity

(*Continued*)

Shirley	• 5 community venues, churches used for events • Few community organisations – 1 per every 3250 residents	*Positives:* • A community organisation with motivated leader and non-local volunteers staffed help centres and support networks • Māori wardens knocked on doors *Negatives:* • Loss of churches, shopping centre and community centre reduced incidental social contact and community capacity • Residents contended that information about available help failed to reach some residents *Negatives:* • Low attendance at events organised by community organisations • Low participation in discussions about the future
Inner City East	• 3 community venues – providing neighbourhood support and access to networking	*Positives:* • Community organisation used arts centre • Continuation of support provided by

(Continued)

Table 8.2 (Cont.)

Name of community	Before the earthquakes	Immediately after	In the medium term (up to 15–17 months after)
	16 community organisations • 10 residents groups	as help centre providing support • Organised community celebrations, commemorations and newsletter *Negatives:* • Loss of housing, churches, social infrastructure reducing incidental social contact	community events to facilitate meetings, events, home visits, networks and communications via various media • Existing venues, organisations and leadership were assets *Negatives:* • Hampered by lack of funds, exhausted staff
***Marae/Ngāi Tahu* (the largest *iwi*/tribe)**	• Well-developed tribal organisation with strong leadership and venues (*marae*) • Provided support – cultural, spiritual, social	*Positives:* • Under auspices of the tribal council overseeing the *iwi's* activities (*Te Rūnanga o Ngai Tahu*), Māori	*Positives/Neutral:* • *Marae* and its community continued to provide support,

(Continued)

- Hosted large groups and equipped to respond to emergency
- Established support programmes for Māori with government and local organisations

- groups and individuals at *Rēhua marae* provided practical, medical, and spiritual support, supplies, shelter, and care to Christchurch's Māori and non-Māori residents
- Māori wardens knocked on doors

e.g. feeding people at own expense

impacts (providing reassurance, reducing fear and isolation, providing a sense of belonging and purpose). Some psychological impacts were also negative as some people expressed feeling burnt out. The provision of support created a post-earthquake culture of innovation and action, thus amplifying community resilience.

- The experience of working together at the community level enhanced community resilience for future adversities (Table 8.3).

We can compare the behaviours and psychological responses that made the four communities more or less socially sustainable before the earthquakes, and those that helped them to respond more or less resiliently afterwards, as in Table 8.4.

3) Community participation in urban planning

Community participation in shaping the built environment can mobilise and empower people through collective action and decision making. It can increase community bonds and attachments, collective capacity and agency (*adaptive capacity*), and simultaneously create places that meet the communities' needs and reinforce their social strengths.

Headline findings

- Communities' experiences of participating in urban planning and/ or interacting with the authorities before the earthquakes could affect their level of participation in planning the rebuild afterwards. Participation depends on a community feeling respected, listened to, and having a belief that it will achieve results. Prior negative experiences limited or hindered participation (e.g. in Shirley).
- People who proactively volunteered and participated in civic events before the earthquakes were more likely to participate in urban planning afterwards.
- Community involvement in decision making and action improved well-being and resilience by giving people a sense of control and determination. Conversely, bureaucratic barriers to collective action negatively impacted well-being and resilience by creating a sense of

Table 8.3 Social capital and cohesion

Name of community	Before the earthquakes	Immediately after the earthquakes	In the medium term (up to 15–17 months after)
Lyttelton	• People knew neighbours • Strong solidarity/community spirit • Community initiative, volunteering and participation in civic activities • Community-level town identity	*Positives:* • Neighbours socialised, providing support • Residents volunteered in relief effort • Residents organised and participated in community events *Neutral:* • Residents questioned legitimacy of community leaders	*Positives:* • Collapsed social divides • Improved community bonds • Enhanced sense of pride in community • Social support • Improved confidence in collective abilities *Negatives:* • Displaced residents suffered from distance from social networks
Shirley	• Deprivation-linked low levels of well-being • Neighbours didn't know each other or communicate • Lack of connections • Lack of trust	*Positives:* • Neighbours, friends, families provided support • A few (but not many) long-term residents helped with community-level mobilisation	*Positives/neutral:* • Social support primarily at individual level, which increased friendliness, caring, reduced social divides, re-ordered priorities

(Continued)

Table 8.3 (Cont.)

Name of community	Before the earthquakes	Immediately after the earthquakes	In the medium term (up to 15-17 months after)
	• Few long-term residents with leadership skills and community values	*Negatives:* • Some residents stayed home out of fear • Lack of volunteers	*Negatives:* • Little collective community action or events • Displaced people leaving reduced sense of community across social divides
Inner City East	• Strong networks • Sense of community • Ethnic diversity - source of strength and part of place-linked community identity	*Positives:* • Residents and neighbours provided support • Residents volunteered in relief effort • Residents attended community events and meetings *Negatives:* • Some people, e.g. Māori, didn't ask for help	*Positives:* • Support, social contact, attendance at social events and community building continued • Support increased, relationships strengthened, social cohesion improved, priorities changed • Area's diversity was a source of strength – varied knowledge to draw upon • Pride enhanced in diversity, community's character and social connections • Stronger sense of community and social connections

(Continued)

		• Existing sense of place kept some residents in area *Negatives:* • Loss of displaced residents reduced trust, increased social problems (caused partially by deprivation) and divisions, reduced sense of community
Marae/Ngāi Tahu (the largest *iwi*/tribe)	• Māori have powerful cultural values for providing support: • *Manaakitanga* – obliges caring and hospitality for all regardless of ethnicity or tribal difference • *Kotahitanga* – uniting to support people regardless of race, culture or ethnic identification	*Positives:* • Māori provided support to each other and wider community • These people felt cared for • Māori participated in group activities, improving support and spiritual well-being, including non-Māori in activities *Negatives:* Some Māori felt unable to ask for help – affecting their ability to provide support	*Positives:* • Māori accommodated displaced family members • The strengths of *tipuna* (ancestors), *whakapapa* (ancestry) and local history of area bolstered commitments to stay in or return to home areas • Providing support reduced isolation, collapsed social and ethnic divides, supported psychological well-being of givers and receivers, strengthened neighbourly connections, increased social contact.

(Continued)

Table 8.3 (Cont.)

Name of community	Before the earthquakes	Immediately after the earthquakes	In the medium term (up to 15-17 months after)
	• *Whanaungatanga* – a sense of family connection developing from kinship rights and obligations – extended to close reciprocal relationships • The strengths of *Tipuna* (ancestors), *whakapapa* (ancestry) and local history of area • *Karakia* – prayer, and *korero* – the opportunity to talk		• Improved community bonds and connections • Enhanced ability to cope *Negatives:* • Some volunteers left exhausted and psychologically affected

Table 8.4 Behaviours and psychological responses that made four communities socially sustainable and resilient

Socially sustainable behaviours and psychological responses	Resilient behaviours and psychological responses
Behaviours:	*Behaviours:*
• Communication and relationships with neighbours • Providing neighbours with support • Strong social networks • Volunteering • Participating in civic organisations • Long length of residence	• Socialising with neighbours • Supporting neighbours • Strong social networks • Volunteering • Participation in community events • Pro-active trusted community leadership who know community well • Community building activities • Social cohesion
Behaviour/psychological response:	
• Self-reliance	
Psychological responses:	*Psychological responses:*
• Social solidarity/community spirit • Pro-community supportive values • Trust in community leadership • Shared place-linked or collective community identity • Sense of pride in the community • Sense of/attachment to place and community	• Positive attitude to diversity • Sense of pride in the community • Sense of/attachment to place and community

powerlessness despite pre-existing community infrastructure and social connections.

• Authorities' failure to incorporate communities' views into redevelopment plans weakened communities' trust in the authorities (Table 8.5).

Concluding comment

This case supports our argument that a socially sustainable community can also be a resilient one when it has ample social resources and strengths. The built environment and community participation in urban development can positively influence and increase these.

Behaviours and psychological responses in resilience case studies

To conclude our case study analyses, Table 8.6 compares the behavioural and psychological dimensions from the 'resilient neighbourhood community framework' with the pro-community behaviours and psychological responses that helped residents of Khulna, Surat, Jakarta, New Orleans and Christchurch to be socially sustainable before floods, a hurricane, an earthquake, cyclones, storm surges and heat waves, *and* respond resiliently during and after them. Surat's informal settlement inhabitants are not included as the data did not link any pro-community behaviours to their flood response, although bonding social capital probably existed among regional groups. Socio-economic/income factors are omitted as these are often, but not always, a barrier to resilience. It is not possible to separate the social strengths displayed before/during/after the adversities out of these few case studies. The social strengths exhibited in communities before each crisis would most likely have existed during and afterwards, and contributed to pro-community outcomes observed at those stages too. Other behaviours and psychological responses were particularly noticeable after the events. Therefore, socially sustainable strengths are also treated as resilient social strengths in this table. It is illustrative rather than exhaustive.

Table 8.5 Community participation

Name of community	Before the earthquakes	Immediately after	In the medium term (up to 15–17 months after)
Lyttelton	• Tradition of volunteering, self-reliance and community action – no information on participation in urban planning	*Positives:* • A week after earthquake in February 2011, residents discussed future of town with community leaders	*Positives:* • 7 weeks after, 400 people attended community meeting organised by local agency to air views for report with recommendations *Negatives:* • Frustration that local board had no power to influence outcome, just report their views • Frustration at red tape hampering community action, and lack of timely communication from authorities
Shirley	• Residents felt overlooked and powerless in dealings with authorities	*Positives/neutral:* • Engaged with authorities on limited basis over essential needs e.g. for public toilets	*Negatives:* • Residents unresponsive at participating in plans for urban regeneration – failed to respond to billboard and text campaigns

(Continued)

Table 8.5 (Cont.)

Name of community	Before the earthquakes	Immediately after	In the medium term (up to 15–17 months after)
		Negatives:	• Authority–community dialogue failed
		• Felt voices were ignored before and after the earthquakes	
Inner City East	• Active community and voluntary life – no information on participation in urban planning	• No information	*Positives:*
			• Residents attended a community meeting
			• Discussed issues, needs and response to earthquake to plan initiatives and input into a City Council Draft Master plan
Marae/Ngāi Tahu (the largest *iwi*/tribe)	• No information available	• No information available	• No information available

Table 8.6 Overall resilient community behaviours and psychological response

Fundamentals of neighbourhood resilience	Behaviours and psychological responses that contributed to community resilience before/during/after adversities
Neighbours that trust one another	*Psychological responses:* • Trust between women (Khulna) • Implied but not mentioned in Surat, Jakarta and Christchurch
Neighbours that interact on a regular basis	*Behaviours:* • Casual social contact (Khulna, New Orleans) • Socialising with neighbours (Khulna, Jakarta, Christchurch) • Strong social networks (Khulna, Surat, Jakarta, Christchurch) • Good communications with neighbours/exchanging news and information with neighbours (Jakarta) • Increased friendliness (Christchurch)
Residents who own their own houses and stay for a while (or rental tenants or informal settlement dwellers that reside in an area for the long-term)	*Behaviours:* • Long length of residence (Surat) • Rapid integration of short-term migrants (Jakarta) • Long length of residence (Christchurch) • Remaining in or returning to local area due to ancestral connections and history (Māori, Christchurch)
Residents with a sense of community (and other psychosocial orientations and attachments towards places and communities)	*Psychological responses:* • Sense of/attachment to place and community (Khulna, Jakarta, Christchurch)

(Continued)

Table 8.6 (Cont.)

Fundamentals of neighbourhood resilience	Behaviours and psychological responses that contributed to community resilience before/during/after adversities
Social cohesion	***Social process encompassing behaviour and psychological responses:*** • Social cohesion (Surat, Jakarta, Christchurch) ***Psychological responses:*** • Positive attitude to population diversity (Surat, Christchurch) • Wide-ranging knowledge of diverse people helpful to response (Christchurch)
Residents who work together for the common good and are involved in community events + Voice and influence (indicator from The Berkeley Group's Social Sustainability Framework), **and civic empowerment** These two categories are amalgamated here as working together for the common good can lead to voice and influence, and civic empowerment	***Behaviours:*** • Community mobilisation (Jakarta, Christchurch) • Volunteering (Christchurch) • Participation in community meetings and events (Christchurch) • Community building activities (Christchurch) • Making sacrifices to improve urban infrastructure (Surat) • Participation in urban planning/ regeneration (Khulna, Surat, Christchurch) • Engaging with authorities (Surat) • Cleaning and maintaining neighbourhood infrastructure, facilities and environment (Jakarta) • Designing a home extension for business activities (Khulna) • Setting up and running a market (Khulna)
Formal and informal places for civic gathering, including flexible use of spaces and alternative spaces	• Community venues and spaces (Surat, New Orleans, Christchurch) • Social facilities on board cruise ships (New Orleans) • Spaces where women do chores and business (Khulna)

Source: Framework adapted from Zautra, Hall, and Murray (2008), applied to our cases by authors.

Notes

1 This was produced by the Asian Cities Climate Change Resilience Network (ACCCRN) initiative with the input of Surat Municipal Corporation and other stakeholders. All Surat material adapted from: *Surat City Resilience Strategy* (2011) unless otherwise indicated in footnotes. There were a limited number of resources available and few discussing social issues.

2 These are overall effects summarised in Asian Cities Climate Change Resilience Network (2011: 2). A wide range of prediction data at city and regional levels is included.

3 Vulnerability to floods was assessed by examining damage from floods, depth of inundation and duration of inundation faced by the households.

4 Stakeholders involved in the creation of Asian Cities Climate Change Resilience Network (2011: 9) include: 'city stakeholders, urban researchers, practitioners and citizens of Surat city'.

5 Shortlength of residence is the opposite of the residential stability dimension of social sustainability and neighbourhood resilience.

6 All Bangladesh case study material adapted from Jabeen (2017).

7 This should not be perceived as negatively judgmental about people in poverty in Surat, merely about their capacity to develop longer-term positive behaviours given the short-term survival challenges they face.

8 All content taken from Asian Cities Climate Change Resilience Network (2011) unless otherwise specified.

9 It should be noted that these better off Surtis had access to services than Surat's slum dwellers, thus improving the conditions under which pro-community behaviours can develop and flourish.

10 All Jakarta material adapted from Wilhelm (2011a, Wilhelm, 2011b).

11 This case shows social unity within shared circumstances of poverty and adversity, and may not be particularly typical of low-income informal settlements.

12 Source: Aisa Tobing, Senior Advisor to the Government, City of Jakarta. Keynote speech given at the MIT Sustainability Summit 2014. http://sustain abilitysummit.mit.edu/programme/#the-collaborative-city

13 All Gulf Coast material adapted from: Spokane, Mori and Martinez (2012).

14 All Christchurch, NZ, material adapted from: Thornley, Ball, Signal, Lawson-Te Aho and Rawson (2013).

15 Practical support included checking on people's well-being, feeding and housing displaced people, allowing public access to water from private wells, distributing food and water to neighbours, and undertaking practical tasks, clearing silt, taking elderly people shopping and repairing property. Emotional support included being together, spontaneous gatherings and backyards and on street corners in the months afterwards, meeting, talking, sharing tea and alcohol, prayer.

References

Achal, SP and Padhya, HJ (2014) 'Rehabilitation of slum: a case study of west zone of Surat City', *International Journal of Engineering Development and Research*

2 (3), accessed on 18 December 2015 at: www.ijedr.org/papers/IJEDR1403001. pdf

Asian Cities Climate Change Resilience Network (2011) *Surat City Resilience Strategy*, accessed in 2014 at: http://acccrn.org/sites/default/files/documents/Sur atCityResilienceStrategy_ACCCRN_01Apr2011_small_0.pdf

Chant, SH and McIlwaine, C (2016) *Cities, Slums and Gender in the Global South: Towards a Feminised Urban Future*, Oxford and New York: Routledge.

Chatterjee, P (2015) 'What Surat learned from a preventable flood', 3 September 2015 *Citiscope Website*, accessed on 18 December 2015 at: http://citiscope.org/ story/2015/what-surat-learned-preventable-flood#sthash.RzQsAXBs.dpuf

Erikson, K (1978) *Everything in its Path: Destruction of Community in the Buffalo Creek Flood*, New York: Simon & Schuster.

Flora (2012) 'Surat: the not-so-little-city that could', *The Accidental Londoner* website/blog, accessed on 23 December 2015 at: www.theaccidentallondoner. com/2012/03/surat-not-so-little-city-that-could.html

Ghanekar, A, Desai, V, Desai, H, Kumar Rathi, S, Acharya, A and Khatri, K (2014) 'Building Resilience to Climate Change and Health: Can Adolescents in Urban Slums be the Answer?', *Asian Journal of Research in Social Sciences and Humanities* 4 (11): 1–15, accessed on 22 December 2015 at: http://uhcrc.org/ sites/uhcrc.org/files/Research%20paper_adolescents%20perspective%20CC% 20and%20health.pdf

Govind, PJ and Verchick, RRM (2015) 'Natural disaster and climate change', in: Alam, S, Atapattu, S, Gonzalez, CG and Razzaque, J (eds), *International Environmental Law and the Global South*, Cambridge: Cambridge University Press, 491–507.

Jabeen, H (2017) 'Gendered space and climate resilience in informal settlements in Khulna city, Bangladesh', unpublished paper. Bangladesh: Department of Architecture, BRAC University.

Loftland, LH (1989) 'Social life in the public realm: a review', *Journal of Contemporary Ethnography*, 17 (4): 453–482.

Spokane, AR, Mori, Y and Martinez, F (2012) 'Considerations in designing transitional communities housing arrays following disasters: Social vulnerability', *Environment and Behaviour* 45: 887–911, accessed on 22 December 2015 at: http://eab.sagepub.com/content/45/7/887

Thornley, L, Ball, J, Signal, L, Lawson-Te Aho, K and Rawson, E (2013) *Building Community Resilience: Learning from the Canterbury Earthquakes*, Report prepared for Health Research Council and Canterbury Medical Research Foundation, Christchurch, accessed on 6 December 2015 at: http://www.quigleyand watts.co.nz/research-and-analysis/Building_Community_Resilience_report-March_2013.pdf?final2

Wilhelm, M (2011a) 'Chapter 5: The role of community resilience in adapting to climate change: The urban poor in Jakarta, Indonesia', in: Otto-Zimmerman, K. (ed.), *Resilient Cities: Cities and Adaptation to Climate Change Proceedings of the Global Forum 2010*, Local Sustainability 1. Springer Science+Business

Media B.V. 45–52, accessed on 22 December 2015 at: http://link.springer.com/content/pdf/10.1007%2F978-94-007-0785-6.pdf

Wilhelm, M (2011b) 'Approaching disaster vulnerability in a megacity: Community resilience to flooding in two Kampungs in Jakarta'. Unpublished Doctoral Dissertation, Achern: University of Passau, accessed on 22 December 2015 at: d-nb.info/1027610234/34

Zautra, A, Hall, J and Murray, K (2008) 'Community development and community resilience: an integrative approach', *Community Development* 39 (3): 130–147.

9 Findings and conclusion

What behavioural and psychological dimensions should developers promote through built environment constructions?

Table 9.1 outlines the dimensions of socially sustainable communities by identifying the dimensions from Dempsey *et al.*'s 'socially sustainable community' framework which overlapped with dimensions from Zautra, Hall and Murray's 'resilient neighbourhood community framework' and were applicable in our case studies (Dempsey, Bramley, Power and Brown, 2009; Zautra, Hall and Murray, 2008). Three new additional dimensions were also identified. Although the two pre-existing frameworks in Tables 4.2 and 5.1 were derived from academic literature,[1] our empirical investigation demonstrated they are applicable in real life developments, and environmental disaster situations. Below are the shared dimensions of social sustainability and resilience that city policymakers, planners and designers should seek to influence through plans, designs, and inclusive, democratic community participation. If further case studies were generated from other projects not considered in this book, they might reveal additional dimensions. However, our list provides a comprehensive if not exhaustive starting point.

Table 9.2 shows the additional dimensions of community resilience that were evident in our case studies.

Further dimensions of community resilience that the urban development and the built environment can also directly influence are in Table 9.3.

Table 9.1 Dimensions of a socially sustainable resilient community

Social sustainability	Community resilience
Pride in and attachment to neighbourhood Dempsey *et al.* Baldwin and King	**Residents with a sense of, attachment to, pride in the place/community** Zautra, Hall and Murray Baldwin and King
Social interaction within the neighbourhood Dempsey *et al.* Baldwin and King	**Neighbours that interact on a regular basis** Zautra, Hall and Murray Baldwin and King
Safety/security (versus risk of crime, antisocial behaviour) Dempsey *et al.* Baldwin and King	**Safety, security and monitoring** Zautra, Hall and Murray Baldwin and King
Stability (versus residential turnover) Dempsey *et al.* Baldwin and King	**Residents who own their own houses and stay for a while** [or rental tenants or informal settlement dwellers that reside in an area for the long-term] Zautra, Hall and Murray Baldwin and King
Participation in collective group/ civic activities Dempsey *et al.* Baldwin and King	**Residents who work together for the common good and are involved in community events** Zautra, Hall and Murray Baldwin and King
Social cohesion Baldwin and King	**Social cohesion** Baldwin and King Zautra, Hall and Murray
Social solidarity/community spirit Baldwin and King	**Social solidarity/community spirit** Baldwin and King
Happiness and well-being Baldwin and King	**Well-being** Baldwin and King
Voice, influence and civic empowerment Baldwin and King	**Voice and influence** Baldwin and King

Source: Authors.

Table 9.2 Additional dimensions of community resilience evident in our examples

Sociable placement of neighbourhoods and facilities, layout of streets	• Physical design of neighbourhood that promotes incidental neighbourly social contact (Khulna, Jakarta) • Centrally located amenities in tent camps (New Orleans) • Spaces for children's play in tent camps (New Orleans) • Main street, Lyttelton, conducive to incidental social contact (Christchurch) • Extensions of private homes where women do business (Khulna)
Social solidarity/community spirit	***Psychological responses:*** • Social solidarity/community spirit (Surat) • Civic commitment (Surat) • Sense of responsibility for the community (Surat) • Pro-community supportive values (Māori, Christchurch) • Community bonds (Christchurch) • Strengthening connections with neighbours (Christchurch)
Strong community organisations, well-connected to the community	• Neighbourhood and community-level organisations providing regular and relief support (Jakarta, Christchurch) • Women's savings group (Khulna)

(Continued)

Strong and trusted community leadership	**Behaviour/psychological response:**
	• Proactive trusted leadership who knew community well (Jakarta, Christchurch)
	• Women leaders pro-active in re-designing neighbourhood spaces (Khulna)
Sense of pride in the place/ community	**Psychological responses:**
	• Sense of pride in the community (Surat, Christchurch)
Sense of belonging	**Psychological response:**
	• Sense of belonging (Surat)
Social support	**Behaviours:**
	• Social support (Surat)
	• Financial and practical support (Jakarta)
	• Emotional, spiritual, social, medical and practical support (Christchurch)
Social order	• Compulsory participation in neighbourhood, enforced sanctions (Jakarta)
Social safety/monitoring	• Tent camps arranged with tent fronts facing others (New Orleans)

(Continued)

Table 9.2 (Cont.)

Identity	***Psychological responses:*** • Place-linked or collective community identity (Surat, Christchurch)
Social integration	***Social processes:*** • Rapid integration of new migrants (Jakarta) • Collapsing social divides (Christchurch)
Collective efficacy, agency, confidence in collective abilities	***Behaviours and psychological responses:*** • Khulna, Jakarta, Christchurch
Re-ordered priorities	***Psychological responses:*** • Christchurch
Well-being	• Positive physical and mental health before the earthquakes contributed to resilience, and was enhanced by pro-community behaviours afterwards (Christchurch)

Source: Authors.

Table 9.3 Additional dimensions of community resilience supported by the built environment

Dimension of community resilience	How the built environment can support/ positively influence it
Physical dimensions	
Flexible use of spaces and alternative spaces	Socially planned physical attribute or organic community solution
Sociable placement of neighbourhoods and facilities, layout of streets	Socially planned physical attribute
Physical features providing protection from weather elements in outdoor 'parochial' and public spaces	Socially planned physical attribute or organic community solution
Social dimensions	
Identity	Built and biophysical environments are key reference points for personal identities
Social integration	Via the visibility and mixing of social groups in public spaces
Collective efficacy, agency, confidence in collective abilities	Cultivated through community participation in urban planning and collective care of infrastructure

Source: Authors.

Conclusion

- This book has followed a simple proposition: *in all societies around the world, our public built environments – public spaces, housing and transport stops – should be planned and designed to promote behaviours and psychological responses that are good for communities, as associated with social capital and cohesion ('pro-community behaviours'). These help communities maintain their quality of life and well-being in routine daily life, and strengthen their resilience to adversity during extraordinary environmental events caused by climate change and other natural disasters.* These two goals are inextricably linked by the common social resources that communities need to achieve both, and should not be addressed separately.
- We sketched out a socially aware planning process whereby: social objectives are incorporated into a building plan, design, and construction through targeted contextual research, community

participation, the use of research data to support culturally and socially appropriate design decisions, and study and assessment methodologies are used to monitor and evaluate both the promised social inputs and achieved social impacts. Pro-community behaviours help to sustain communities: through the ways that networks operate, people conduct relationships, organise themselves and take action, as motivated and mediated by psychological strengths such as bonds, pride, sense of responsibility, sense of/attachment to place and community and so on. There are established links between social capital and cohesion, health and well-being, which improve quality of life, and daily social sustainability (Ferlander, 2007; Berkman, 2000). Similarly, to prepare for, survive, recover from and adapt after environmental adversities ('resilience'), urban communities need to maintain and develop their social capital and social cohesion, and associated pro-community outcomes. Adaptive capacity relies on members' abilities to band together and achieve shared objectives. People need the capacity, but also the self-efficacy and agency to be propelled into action. Resilience is both a practical and well-being issue for individuals and communities.

- Urban form and social infrastructure have a critical influence on a community's sustainability and resilience. The built environment contributes to an enabling total environment for the development of social capital and social cohesion. When designed with social goals, its users are more likely to develop strong social resources, connect with places and spaces, and use them flexibly when their form is changed by an adversity. Resilience includes transformative qualities such as reconfiguring a physical place to serve current community needs. A place is only as effective as the way people use it.

- Places, spaces and amenities that have positive social and health effects are more likely to retain residents willing to invest in them both socially and financially and stay long-term, raising quality of life. Early investment in socially aware planning takes longer, but creates buy-in and support that saves on the heavier cost of a failing development that does not meet local needs or have a positive social influence. Social sustainability is important because without strong networked, cohesive communities, the human capital required to build, run and maintain sustainable, resilient cities will wither. The health and well-being of populations contributes to strong economies and societies, and better human capacity to work with contemporary urban and environmental challenges. As well as human benefits, there are economic and commercial benefits. A more resilient community that can help look after itself and its city after unplanned adversities makes the initial investment in socially aware planning cost-effective, in respect of rebuilding costs in locations vulnerable to climate change-related impacts and natural disasters. This planning will help create the conditions under which organic solutions will emerge, and make our communities, and the investments within them, more vibrant, resilient and longer-lasting.

• Ours is not a complex argument but a powerful one in a climate where the social dimension of sustainability and resilience remains sorely neglected, and a topic that appears to befuddle policy and planning officers lacking expertise in behavioural and psychological social matter, and intangible social processes. We have sought to de-mystify these concepts and lay out a practical process that can be followed in any country. Chapter 10 offers a concrete set of recommendations that can be implemented, drawing on the approaches, tools and methods shown in this book. We urge the policy, planning and development sectors to help communities worldwide respond to urgent urban and environmental challenges by implementing socially aware planning and design for sustainability and resilience.

Note

1 Dempsey *et al.*'s (2009) framework was based on theoretical and practitioner perspectives.

References

Berkman, LF (2000) 'Social support, social networks, social cohesion and health', *Social Work in Health Care* 31 (2): 3–14.

Dempsey, N, Bramley, G, Power, S and Brown, C (2009) 'The social dimension of sustainable development: Defining urban social sustainability', *Sustainable Development* 19: 289–300.

Ferlander, S (2007) 'The importance of different forms of social capital for health', *Acta Sociologa* 50: 115–128.

Zautra, A, Hall, J and Murray, K (2008) 'Community development and community resilience: an integrative approach', *Community Development* 39 (3): 130–147.

10 Recommendations

Planning and designing for the socially sustainable, resilient community

The big picture

Rapid urbanisation due to economic growth and population expansion puts pressure on available land, urban infrastructure, and green space, and is occurring faster than governments or the market can provide safely-located, adequate housing or public infrastructure for their growing populations. Climate change can place additional environmental stress on urban infrastructure and populations. This is especially true in developing countries, and those with large numbers of people in poverty who tend to live in the most vulnerable locations and structures. Sustainable approaches to urban development provide an urban design approach that responds to these tensions applied in a resource aware context. However, they alone will not suffice. While implementation of plans and high-quality construction is crucial, the human dimension of attention to social sustainability and resilience is also essential.

Sub-standard housing and infrastructure pose risks to the social sustainability of communities, and the collective social capacity of a neighbourhood to cope with natural disasters and/or climate change, hence its resilience. A well-built physical environment and infrastructure, designed with social interaction in mind, can increase the social sustainability and resilience of communities.

Recommendations

Stage 1: scheme conception and real estate pre-development

Applicable everywhere

Social sustainability and community resilience are important – perhaps even more important in developing as well as developed countries.

Case example:
Our cases cover all continents: North and South America, Africa, Europe, Asia and Australasia.

Recommendation:
Planners and developers in all countries should incorporate the social dimension of planning and design for sustainability and resilience into urban development and construction.

Integration

Expert and technological approaches to urban planning can overlook the dynamic growth in a city and fail to consider unpredictable demographic and micro-level community trends and dynamics, and how the built environment can support these. Solutions to resilience that begin with technology rather than people often fall into this trap, and may not suit the community they are inserted into without being co-designed. Residents' and users' strategies for social organisation and life management should be explored during scheme conception, and respected in plans and designs. Designs should enhance social resources and special local strengths such as networks, safety and community bonds. These are important for quality of life, health and well-being in all countries and cities, but especially in social environments where there is a history of division, tension, crime and violence, or areas that are subject to climate change impacts and/or frequent natural disasters.

Case example:
Communities in Buenos Aires, Delhi, Cape Town, Portland and Manchester took part in civic and social activities that involved engaging with built environment spaces in ways that fostered connections in 'normal' times. Communities in Jakarta, Surat and Christchurch employed micro-level social strategies to support each other, and manage and renew their physical environments after disasters.

Recommendation:
City governments and developers should integrate and jointly address physical and social sustainability and resilience through planning and design by devising and implementing clear social objectives.

Respectful of change impacts

Developments can cause unintended impacts to the existing social environment, health and well-being of a community. For example, the relocation of a population may adversely affect key social networks as well as livelihood possibilities

Case example:
The residents of Caballito, Buenos Aires, contested the building of isolationist tower blocks that had adverse impacts on neighbourly relations in their tight-knit community. Poor people living in the informal settlements of Surat and Jakarta who were moved to alternative accommodation had a tendency to return if they found life harder.

Recommendation:
Developments should take the impact of changes to the existing social fabric into account from the start and devise schemes that address social needs and provide social benefits.

Stage 2: research and community participation

Research

Planners and designers should collaborate with social scientists to examine and understand a neighbourhood's social environment, its complexity, diversity, and dynamics, and the physical, economic and political context, so as to act with sensitivity when planning and building a development project. The physical environment can have different social and cultural meanings for residents and users, especially in places with a complex and divisive urban history. The design or development of new or existing sites may affect these meanings.

Case example:
Social scientists analysed the symbolic urban landscape in Belfast so that developers could build progressive accommodation without exacerbating tensions through poorly informed design. Social scientists devised an assessment framework for the Berkeley Group to measure the social sustainability of designs for new housing communities.

Recommendations:

- Those involved with development should employ social researchers to use context-appropriate research methods – both qualitative/ethnographic for depth of perspectives and quantitative for trends in perspectives – to document the local context.
- Local stakeholders must be consulted: government sector, civil

(Continued)

(Cont.)

Research

- society, business owners, pro-gramme financiers – local voices with key knowledge about the local context and any social pro-blems, such as violence and crime, that could be addressed through an urban development.
- The blend of research data, and professional and community per-spectives, offers the most holistic and powerful evidence base for informing socially sustainable designs.

Community participation and input

Community participation and input in the urban development and design process, including risk analysis, can help communities and developers identify the social aspects that developments need to consider and or accommodate. This allows them to collaborate on ways of enhancing positive aspects (e.g. social mixing) and improving or minimising negative aspects (e.g. crime) through design and con-struction, as well as giving the community a sense of ownership in improving the urban environment. This is especially important in informal settlements, where establishing proactive neighbourhood organisations, or strengthening those that already exist, and ensuring that they are included in the development, implementa-tion, and monitoring of plans and programmes can improve the quality of life. This occurs through the development of social bonds, social support and increased community spirit.

Case example:
Communities in Khayelitsha, Cape Town, helped identify trends in crime and violence so that design elements were incorporated in regeneration that created opportunities for surveillance. These have drastically reduced crime rates.

Recommendation:
Community participation is an inherent and essential aspect of urban develop-ment, and should always be included in socially planned projects. In order to pre-pare for effective community participa-tion, as well as ensuring that professionals are open to receiving and incorporating inputs, capacity building may be required on both sides.

Timing of participatory studies and assessments

Studies such as Social Sustainability and Community Resilience Assessments, Health Impact Assessments (HIAs), Social Impact Assessments (SIAs), and Co-Design projects should be started soon after the idea for a scheme is conceptualised. These studies should be able to influence plans and not be delayed until after they are finalised or a development constructed.

Case example:
Berkeley Group apply their social sustainability framework in the pre-development phase during the design process as part of planning applications.

Recommendation:
Those involved in development (including government officials approving plans) should insist on early research and participatory studies.

Understanding existing needs, resources and strengths

All communities have specific *needs* or *weaknesses* – absent resources and strengths that developments can address. They also have *social resources* such as social capital and cohesion, and social equity. Their *social strengths* are specifically local manifestations of the dimensions of these concepts or other closely related attributes. For example, the identities of places and people may be an outcome of social capital. Ignoring or undermining a community's existing social strengths can lead to the unexpected restriction or failure of a development, with negative business impacts for investors. Plans and designs for new places or the renewal of existing ones can scrutinise how they can fit with or enhance, for example, a shared sense of place or attachment to a place, or individual or collective identities linked to a place.

Case example:
Cape Town's VPUU project mapped community needs and social organisational patterns within land spaces designated for renovation. Developers in Caballito, Buenos Aires, failed to consider the impacts of tall tower blocks on existing neighbourly relations and social capital in the streets where these were built. Residents hence found a way to prove that these developments were unsustainable which led to new restrictions on building.

Recommendation:
Developers and others involved with the development should collaborate with social scientists and the community to conduct resource or 'asset' mapping exercises to document and understand needs (weaknesses), resources and strengths, and match them with development possibilities.

Social capital and cohesion are vital resources

Urban development should promote the emergence or enhancement of these social resources by, for example, encouraging neighbourhood interactions and networks, and social mixing and collaboration among demographically diverse residents. Local people should be given opportunities to participate in community-level civil society and civic activities, including participatory planning, co-design, and maintenance of infrastructure which strengthen a community's governance or sense of ownership of their infrastructure. These increase their vested interest in improving, protecting and restoring their urban environment after a crisis.

Case example:
Residents of the village of Santa Ana, Paraguay, cultivated and maintained strong social capital and cohesion by collaborating on the maintenance of their infrastructure. Residents of Inner City East, Lyttleton and Māori communities in or near Christchurch had strong traditions of volunteering and civic activity before the earthquakes, which meant that substantial numbers helped their communities and used spaces innovatively afterwards.

Recommendation:
Architects, planners and developers should intentionally investigate ways of promoting social capital and cohesion through designs, public and local organisations' participation in the governance and ownership of infrastructure.

Knowing the community characteristics that promote social cohesion

Knowing which demographic characteristics bind some people, for example, long length of residence and income equality, may illuminate those which divide others. These characteristics may vary by location. Less competition between diverse people may result in more personal investment in a place. Stronger social capital and cohesive community relationships better equip community members to behave resiliently.

Case example:
Surat's long-term, middle-income residents were able to act collectively to support the city during ordinary life and crises, despite being regionally and ethnically diverse.

Recommendation:
Urban programmes should analyse the state of social cohesion, and target fragmented populations with urban projects that build social capital and cohesion. Intra-group participation in urban schemes can help build a common sense of purpose, social solidarity and community spirit.

Socio-demographic diversity as a source of strength

Although socio-demographic diversity is sometimes a challenge to urban social cohesion, cohesion can be a strength for socially aware planning. Diverse people represent a variety of perspectives and interests. When they participate in development, they can identify more needs, resources, strengths, possible inputs, impacts and longer-term outcomes. Cities that cater to multiple perspectives and interests may attract wider investment. Diverse perspectives, interests, skills and values can mean more resources and strengths to draw upon during crises.

Case example:
The ethnically diverse inhabitants of Christchurch's Inner City East neighbourhood regarded their diversity and cohesion as a source of pride that motivated a collective response after the earthquakes. The Māori population had cultural values of caring and hospitality that compelled them to help all people regardless of background.

Recommendation:
Those involved with development should embrace rather than fear socio-demographic diversity when approaching a new community, and harness multiple perspectives to their full advantage.

Equitable access to climate-protective and sociable locations and spaces for all gender statuses

The social conditions and behavioural norms of physical places influence the presence of women, men and people with non-binary gender identities. Spaces need to be safe, secure and compel people to develop a sense of belonging in order to attract all gender statuses to populate them in trouble-free times. If local behavioural norms spatially segregate gender groups, these may feature sub-optimal protection from adverse weather elements. Equitable access to safe, well-protected spaces that offer social network-building opportunities for all gender statuses are an essential design aspect for resilience. They ensure that communities have the maximum available social and human capacity to cope with and adapt to climate change.

Case example:
Cape Town's VPUU project implemented design features and street patrols that reduced the crime rate so significantly that the whole community was able to populate and enjoy the public realm. Trauma counselling for women bonded participants so closely that the whole community designed public art, growing its collective social capacity. The women

Recommendation:
Urban development stakeholders and neighbourhood organisations should collaborate with residents, especially women and people with non-binary gender identities, to map and understand the locations and spaces that they frequent, and how these are different from those used by men. Development stakeholders must uphold and implement a principle of the

(*Continued*)

(Cont.)

Equitable access to climate-protective and sociable locations and spaces for all gender statuses

and men of Khulna, Bangladesh, lived their lives in separate physical spaces for large parts of their time. Some such locations disadvantaged women by isolating them, exposing them to greater climate hazards, and equipping them less well with protective features. Whilst engaged with their physical surroundings, women were empowered when they had opportunities to provide input into community design situations.

equitable distribution of well-protected places for all gender status in plans for resilient infrastructure. Where people have self-built protective features, they must be supported to enhance or maintain these. Formal and informal development initiatives should find ways of shifting gender norms so that all gender statuses can mix safely and comfortably in communal physical spaces to increase collective capacity for resilience, and women have equitable opportunities to influence design outcomes.

Principles of participatory planning and co-design

There should be shared objectives that inspire all key sector stakeholders to give their input. These objectives should be remembered throughout the programme.

Case example:
Cape Town's VPPU aimed to design out crime and promote community and economic development, and sustainability, which inspired and motivated the community and professional stakeholders alike.

All social and cultural groups present in an area should be consulted and given opportunities to participate in the development. Minority perspectives, for example, those of indigenous people, ethnic, religious and economic minorities should be included.

Case example:
Māori people offered socially impactful suggestions for the proposed Bus Xchange upgrade in Christchurch.

Adopting a democratic ethos and participatory or community-led approaches to development are the most successful methods of building trust with a community.

Case example:
Community members who participated in Cape Town's VPUU project, and the restoration of public square and spaces in Portland and Manchester were encouraged by a democratic ethos and decision-making styles.

(Continued)

(Cont.)

Principles of participatory planning and co-design

Co-design interventions should appeal to a wide demographic through transparent, accountable processes, and community outreach and education programmes. Ideally, economic opportunities should also emerge.

Case example:
Cape Town's VPUU embodied inclusive principles and methods, a successful feedback mechanism, and participatory and income generation options for community members.

When co-design schemes are conceived, their organisers should aim to combine the urban development project with community development, and think of broader outcomes for communities, for example, the creation of economic opportunities as project spin-offs.

Case example:
Portland residents who regenerated public squares improved their mental well-being and social capital through participation, strengthening their community. Cape Town's VPUU project provided stalls for traders and employment for inhabitants in managing amenities. The city's redesigned central railway station offered informal vendors the opportunity to sell produce in a dedicated roof-top space.

Recommendation:
Planners, architects, and developers should design projects adopting these participatory and co-design principles.

Resource mapping for resilience

- In areas vulnerable to adverse weather events and natural disasters, urban development leaders should commission social scientists to document and analyse communities' social resources and strengths, and how these intertwine with physical resources on a routine, ongoing basis as part of City Sustainability and Resilience Strategies.
- A pre-crisis record of where people live should be created, so that supportive social groupings may be allocated post-crisis housing together. This may preserve and strengthen existing social capital, social support and collective efficacy.
- Records should be kept up to date, so they can be consulted during the planning of post-crisis housing and rebuilding.
- The micro-scale social and community adaptation strategies employed by urban residents need to be documented before and after crises so that they may be enhanced by formal and macro-level strategies.

(*Continued*)

(Cont.)

Resource mapping for resilience

- Providing, maintaining, cultivating and restoring physical and social resources should be addressed jointly after a crisis.
- The health impacts of collapsing community structures and resources, and social solutions provided by different forms of temporary and transitional housing should both be recorded. Health impacts can be more persuasive than social ones at a policy level.

Case example:
Jakarta's *kampung* communities adopted their own micro-level collaborative strategies to cope with flooding, as enhanced by formal neighbourhood organisations. The lessons that emerged from the Gulf Coast case as regards the separation of key social support networks after a disaster shows the importance of pre-disaster records for highlighting social groupings.

Recommendation:
Urban development leaders and developers planning for social and physical resilience should adopt these principles.

Community relationships with planning and city authorities

Pre-existing mutual trust and respect between authorities and communities are important. Communities who have positive experiences of participating in development and planning before a crisis are more likely to participate in one afterwards. Participation will help a community to heal from the trauma of losing their built environment if they can contribute to re-envisaging and restoring it. This is particularly so of the sensitive restoration of buildings or city places that formed reference points for a shared sense of place or attachment to a place, or personal or group identities. The results of participatory processes and consultations should be made public as soon as possible. A lack of transparency and incorporation of public input will weaken trust in authorities.

Case example:
The 'Surtis' of Surat had a positive relationship with the local authorities through 'normal' and 'crisis' times. Residents of Lyttleton near Christchurch had a strong civic culture and community leadership before the

Recommendation:
Local authorities should invite public participation in rebuilding and restoration at the earliest possible opportunity, and act transparently and reliably regarding the findings and decision-making resulting from participation.

(*Continued*)

(Cont.)

Community relationships with planning and city authorities

---

earthquakes, and large numbers gave immediate input into post-disaster planning. However, Shirley residents experienced a history of mistrust and negative dealings with local authorities, so engaged minimally or failed to respond afterwards.

Stage 3: design decisions and implementation

Evidence-based decision making

Evidence-based design solutions can have a strong impact. The intended outcome of a design decision should be envisaged when made, and supported by evidence and advice from the community and experts.

Case example:
Cape Town's VPUU project involved experts and the community in analysing violence and crime problems, and accordingly designed walkways, public spaces and surveillance buildings that resulted in a colossal reduction in crime levels. Social scientists in Belfast used qualitative and ethnographic social research methods to collect evidence of the local interpretation of the urban landscape to inform careful design decisions.

Recommendation:
Planners and developers should ensure design decisions have been guided by robust supporting evidence of their likely social impacts.

Design principles

Site locations and design features should be selected that may enhance existing positive social resources, and also create new ones. Design features with a positive impact in one place may not have the same impact elsewhere.

(*Continued*)

(Cont.)

Design principles

Case example:
Social scientists in Belfast recommended that developers located the entrances to a housing complex in neutral spaces in a sectarianised urban landscape to promote social cohesion between tenants. Row houses (known as terraced houses in the UK) were not a universal design solution for neighbourly communications, promoting it in Buenos Aires but not in Delhi.

Recommendation:
Planners and designers should go beyond utilitarian design to create places and infrastructure that serves residents' or users' social and cultural needs, rather than just meeting financial or engineering requirements.

Mixed neighbourhoods

Planners and designers should build mixed land-use and demographically mixed neighbourhoods with open space at neighbourhood and precinct level to promote intra-group mixing and bridging social capital between social groups, by age, ethnicity, socio-economic status and so on. Mixed income and mixed-use development is more socially and environmentally sustainable, but often requires non-market financial assistance to ensure economic sustainability.

Case example:
Residents of several mixed-use neighbourhoods in Delhi, where block housing was built around or near communal spaces, interacted and cultivated neighbourly relationships in the spaces and lively streets.

Recommendation:
Developers and planners should support mixed neighbourhoods to the best of their ability, and seek ways of sustaining such developments in the longer term.

Housing with social infrastructure

Social spaces and infrastructure are critical to the development of social capital and cohesion in new housing developments, in addition to the placement and design of dwelling units. High density, well-structured residences with adequate spaces and facilities can support the increase of feelings of safety, and higher levels of trust.

(Continued)

(Cont.)

Housing with social infrastructure

Case example:
Berkeley Group use their Social Sustainability Assessment Framework to assess the effectiveness of new developments, which gives residents a chance to offer feedback on their experiences. This information is used to constantly re-evaluate new design features.

Recommendation:
Developers should build housing with well-integrated social infrastructure and social spaces, with government planners requiring such spaces for approvals.

Minimise relocation and upheaval

Temporary and transitional housing should be allocated in ways that keep bonded neighbours and cultural groups together. It should be arranged so that shared social spaces are provided between the units that facilitate social contact.

Case example:
The relocation of informal settlement dwellers in Surat and Jakarta, and Gulf Coast residents into temporary accommodation after a hurricane demonstrated that unless key social groupings and resources were preserved, these housing allocations could have adverse impacts.

Recommendation:
Government officials should aim to keep dislocated communities together. Relocation areas will require even better and more social infrastructure and social spaces.

Consider incremental housing

Incremental housing should be considered to provide a basic structure and allow individuals to improve incrementally or progressively as resources permit. Existing neighbourhood social structures and networks can survive and thrive if built upon existing housing sites.

Case example:
Experts who observed how communities fared in socially inadequate post-disaster housing in the Gulf Coast case made a strong case for the health and economic benefits of building on existing sites.

Recommendation:
Policies should allow for and promote incremental housing.

Need for community space

Communities need places and spaces for incidental social contact, and physical venues and spaces for events that bring groups of community members together. Safety and security is improved in spaces with a lively presence of demographically diverse people, which in turn improves levels of trust in others. Social mixing between diverse groups is a starting point for economic and social equity and inclusion. After a crisis, communities must be allowed to use alternative spaces to meet their social and housing needs – otherwise the social health of the community and psychological health of individuals will suffer.

Case example:
In Delhi, block housing with internal and nearby external public spaces supported neighbourly relations through incidental and organised social contact. The Portland public squares case showed how these can be used in 'normal' times, while the Christchurch case showed the need for flexible and creative uses of spaces in emergencies.

Recommendation:
Planners, architects and developers should ensure that all neighbourhood developments include well-located and accessible public spaces and promote multi-purpose, flexible usages.

Transport stops

Transport stops are distinctive features of urban areas and create a meeting-place and interchange for large numbers of people as well as serving as a connection point for transport services. They are city places in their own right, and the spaces around and within them are sometimes overlooked areas that can be utilised to promote improved interaction between people, as well as strengthen a place's identity and offer livelihood possibilities.

Case example:
Cape Town's central railway station was redesigned to provide spaces for the city's residents to mix and for informal trade. A pre-development consultation proposed that Christchurch's Bus Xchange included spaces for performances and socialising.

Recommendation:
Planners and designers should think beyond the utilitarian and commercial uses of transport stops and utilise the social and place-making opportunities provided by the internal and external spaces within and around them for positive social impacts. They should integrate the sociability and visibility of people, and the beneficial effects that places can have on well-being into their designs.

Equitable access

Poorer people shouldn't be located on the fringes of a city, but given equitable access to its advantages, and key spaces.

Case example:
The spaces around Cape Town's central railway station were located near to low-income settlements and were designed to allow poorer people to congregate and sell produce in them.

Recommendation:
City officials, planners and developers should ensure that affordable and accessible housing and public spaces for congregation and recreation are located within a reasonable distance of a city's key economic opportunities and amenities to democratise access.

Stage 4: monitoring and evaluation

Community participation in monitoring and evaluation

Community members who participate in the initial and ongoing monitoring or evaluation of schemes, particularly when they have contributed, can develop a sense of ownership and empowerment that raises the likelihood of becoming psychologically invested in a place, and feeling motivated to take care of it. Communities affected by crises should participate in monitoring and evaluation of plans and restoration projects themselves to bring their concerns to the relevant authorities, and also experience psychological healing through witnessing and participating in the recovery process.

Case example:
Researchers in Delhi, Portland, Manchester, Yala, and the UK's Berkeley Group blended qualitative and quantitative methods to evaluate the social sustainability, health and well-being effects of housing developments and public squares and parks. Cape Town's VPUU project gave Khayelitsha residents the chance to carry out an ongoing evaluation survey themselves.

Recommendation:
Developers and government officials should ensure that communities as well as experts conduct and deliver monitoring and evaluation exercises to maximise opportunities for empowerment.

References

Achal, SP and Padhya, HJ (2014) 'Rehabilitation of slum: a case study of west zone of Surat City', *International Journal of Engineering Development and Research* 2 (3): accessed on 18 December 2015 at: www.ijedr.org/papers/IJEDR1403001. pdf

Adelaide City Council (2005) *Social Sustainability Partnership Agreement*, accessed on 23 December 2015 at: www.adelaidecitycouncil.com/assets/acc/Community/planning-programmes/docs/social_sustainability_partnership_agreement.pdf

Adger, WN (2000) 'Social and ecological resilience: Are they related?' *Progress in Human Geography* 24: 347–364.

Adger, WN (2003) 'Social capital, collective action, and adaptation to climate change', *Economic Geography* 79 (4): 387–404.

AECOM for CDP/Bloomberg Philanthropies and C40 Cities (2014) *Protecting our Capital: How Climate Adaptation in Cities Creates a Resilient Place for Business*, accessed on 23 December 2015 at: www.cdp.net/CDPResults/CDP-global-cities-report-2014.pdf

Aked, J, Thompson, S, Marks, N and Cordon, C (2008) *Five Ways to Well-being: The Evidence*, London: New Economics Foundation (NEF).

Allan, P, Byant, M, Wirsching, C, Garcia, D and Rodriguez, MT (2013) 'The influence of urban morphology on the resilience of cities following an earthquake', *Journal of Urban Design* 18 (2): 242–262.

Almedom, A (2004) 'Factors that mitigate war-induced anxiety and mental distress', *Journal of Biosocial Science* 36: 445–461.

Anderson, J, Ruggeri, K, Steemers, K and Huppert, F (2016) 'Lively social space, well-being activity, and urban design', *Environment and Behaviour*, 1–32: accessed at: http://journals.sagepub.com/doi/abs/10.1177/0013916516659108

Appadurai, A (2001) 'Deep democracy: Urban governability and the horizon of politics', *Environment and Urbanization* 13 (2): 23–43.

Asian Cities Climate Change Resilience Network (2011) *Surat City Resilience Strategy*, accessed in 2014 at: http://acccrn.org/sites/default/files/documents/SuratCityResilienceStrategy_ACCCRN_01Apr2011_small_0.pdf

Bach, R, Doran, R, Gibb, L, Kaufman, D and Settle, K (2010) 'Policy Challenges in Supporting Community Resilience', Working Paper for the Multinational

Community Resilience Policy Group (Co-chaired by US and UK), London, accessed on 6 December 2015 at: www.fema.gov/media-library/assets/docu ments/21050?id=4563

Bacon, N, Cochrane, D and Woodcraft, S (2012) *Creating Strong Communities: How to Measure the Social Sustainability of New Housing Development*, Berkeley Housing Group, accessed on 23 December 2015 at: www.berkeleygroup.co. uk/media/pdf/7/8/berkeley-reports-and-opinions-social-sustainability-reports-creating-strong-communities-part-one.pdf

Baldwin, C (2012) *Locating Britishness? Mediating identity, ethnicity, community and place in multi-ethnic Swindon.* Unpublished DPhil thesis. Oxford: University of Oxford.

Baldwin, C (2015), 'Assessing impacts on people's relationships to place and community in health impact assessment: an anthropological approach'. *Impact Assessment and Project Appraisal (IAPA)* 33 (2): 154–159.

Barata-Salgeuiro, T and Erkip, F (2014) 'Retail planning and urban resilience: an introduction to the special issue', *Cities* 36: 107–111.

Barbieri, P, Russell, H, and Paugam, S (1999) 'Social capital and exits from unemployment', unpublished paper, OECD.

Beard, VA, A Mahendra, and MI Westphal (2016) 'Towards a More Equitable City: Framing the Challenges and Opportunities'. Working Paper. World Resources Report. Washington, DC: World Resources Institute.

Berger-Schmitt, R (2000) 'Social Cohesion as an Aspect of the Quality of Societies: Concept and Measurement', Center for Survey Research and Methodology (ZUMA), EU Report Working Paper no. 14, Mannheim, Germany.

Berkeley Group (2014) *Creating Successful Places: A Toolkit*, accessed on 6 December 2015 at: www.berkeleygroup.co.uk/media/pdf/l/h/berkeley-social-sus tainability-toolkit.pdf

Berkeley Group website (n.d.) accessed in 2014-2015 at: www.berkeleygroup.co. uk/sustainability/social-sustainability/creating-successful-places

Berkes, F and Ross, H (2012) 'Community resilience: Toward an integrated approach, *Society and Natural Resources: An International Journal* 26 (1): 5–20.

Berkes, F, Colding, J and Folke, C (2003) *Navigating Social–ecological Systems: Building Resilience for Complexity and Change*, Cambridge: Cambridge University Press.

Berkman, LF (2000) 'Social support, social networks, social cohesion and health', *Social Work in Health Care* 31 (2): 3–14.

Bidwell, S, and Dell, R (2011) *Long-term Planning for Recovery after Disasters: Ensuring Health in All Policies*, Christchurch, NZ: Canterbury District Health Board, accessed on 22 December 2015 at: www.cph.co.nz/files/LTPRecovery-HIAP-fulldocument.pdf

Blackman, T (2006) *Placing Health: Neighbourhood Renewal, Health Improvement and Complexity*, Bristol, UK: Policy.

Bond, S and Thompson-Fawcett, M (2007) 'Public participation and New Urbanism: a conflicting agenda?' *Planning Theory and Practice* 8 (4): 449–472.

Bourdieu, P (1985) 'The forms of capital', in: Richardson, JG (ed.), *Handbook for Theory and Resarch for the Sociology of Education*, New York: Greenwood: 241–258.

Bramley, G and Power, S (2009) 'Urban form and social sustainability: the role of density and housing type', *Environment and Planning B: Planning and Design* 36: 30–48.

Bramley, G, Dempsey, N, Power, S, Brown, C and Watkins, D (2009) 'Social sustainability and urban form: Evidence from five British cities', *Environment and Planning A* 41: 2125–2142.

Brown, JS, Learmonth, AM and Mackereth, CJ (2015) *Promoting Public Mental Health and Well-being: Principles into Practice*, London: Jessica Kingsley.

Caistor, L (2013) 'Losing the plot in Buenos Aires', *The Social Life of Cities: Stories about Urban Innovation*, London: Social Life, accessed on 22 December 2015 at: www.social-life.co/publication/Social_Life_of_Cities_stories/

Calthorpe, P (1993) *The Next American Metropolis: Ecology, Community, and the American Dream*, New York: Princeton Architectural Press.

Cantle, T (2001) *Community Cohesion: A Report of the Independent Review Team*, London: Home Office.

Carpenter, A (2013) *Resilience in the Social and Physical Realms: Lessons from the Gulf Coast*, Background Paper prepared for the *Global Assessment Report on Disaster Risk Reduction 2013*, Geneva: The United Nations Office for Disaster Risk Reduction (UNISDR) and Global Assessment Report on Disaster Risk Reduction (GAR), accessed on 6 December 2015 at: www.preventionweb.net/english/hyogo/gar/2013/en/bgdocs/Carpenter,%202013.pdf

CARRI (2013) *Definitions of Community Resilience: An Analysis*. A CARRI Report, Community and Regional Resilience Institute, accessed on 23 December 2015 at: www.resilientus.org/wp-content/uploads/2013/08/definitions-of-community-resilience.pdf

Cave, B (2015) 'Assessing the potential health effects of policies, plans, programmes and projects', in Barton, H, Thompson, S, Burgess, S and Grant, M (eds), *The Routledge Handbook of Planning for Health and Well-being*, London: Routledge.

Cervero, R (1998) *The Transit Metropolis*, Washington, DC: Island Press.

Chambers, R and Conway, G (1992) 'Sustainable Rural Livelihoods: Practical Concepts for the 21st Century'. Sussex Discussion Paper 296, Brighton, UK: Institute of Development Studies.

Chant, SH and McIlwaine, C (2016) *Cities, Slums and Gender in the Global South: Towards a Feminised Urban Future*, Oxford and New York: Routledge.

Chatterjee, P (2015) 'What Surat learned from a preventable flood', 3 September 2015 *Citiscope Website*, accessed on 18 December 2015 at: http://citiscope.org/story/2015/what-surat-learned-preventable-flood#sthash.RzQsAXBs.dpuf

Chen, LC, Liu, YC, Chan, KC (2006) 'Integrated community-based disaster management programme in Taiwan: A case study of Shang-An Village', *Natural Hazards* 37 (1–2): 209–223.

Cobb, S (1976) 'Social support as a moderator of life stress', *Journal of Psychosomatic Medicine* 38: 300–313.

Cohen, S and Syme, SDL (1985) *Social Support and Health*, London: Academic Press.

Colantonio, A (2008) 'Traditional and Emerging Prospects in Social Sustainability in Measuring Social Sustainability: Best Practice from Urban Renewal in the EU 2008/02', EIBURS Working Paper Series November 2008. 1–27, accessed on 23 December 2015 at: http://oisd.brookes.ac.uk/sustainable_communities/resources/SocialSustainabilityProspectspaper.pdf

Colantonio, A and Dixon, T (2010) *Urban Regeneration and Social Sustainability: Best Practice from European Cities*, Oxford: John Wiley & Sons.

Coleman JS (1988a) 'Social capital in the creation of human capital', *American Journal of Sociology* 94: S95–121.

Coleman JS (1988b) 'The creation and destruction of social capital: implications for the law', *Notre Dame Journal of Law, Ethics, Public Policy* 3: 375–404.

Coleman, JS (1990) *Foundations of Social Theory*, Cambridge, MA and London: The Belknap Press of Harvard University Press.

Collins Dictionary Online Version, accessed on 3 January 2016 at: www.collinsdictionary.com

Cooper, M (2006) *Social Sustainability in Vancouver*. Research Report F62. Ottawa: Family Network. Canadian Policy Research Networks, accessed on 23 December 2015 at: http://rcrpp.org/documents/45693_en.pdf

Council of Europe/European Commission for Social Cohesion (CDCS) (2004) *Revised Strategy for Social Cohesion*, Strasbourg: CDCS.

Coutts, A, Ramos Pinto, P, Cave, B and Kawachi, I (2007) *Social Capital Indicators in the UK: A Research Project for the Commission for Racial Equality*, Leeds and London: Ben Cave Associates and Commission for Racial Equality.

Cox, RS and Perry, KE (2011) 'Like a fish out of water: Reconsidering disaster recovery and the role of place and social capital in community disaster resilience', *American Journal of Community Psychology* 48: 395–411.

Danna, K and Griffin, RW (1999) Health and well-being in the workplace: a review and synthesis of the literature, *Journal of Management* 25 (3): 357–384.

da Silva, J and Morera, B (2014) *City Resilience Index: City Resilience Framework*. Ove Arup and Partners International Limited and The Rockefeller Foundation, accessed on 23 December 2015 at: http://publications.arup.com/Publications/C/City_Resilience_Framework.aspx

Davoudi, S, Shaw, S, Haider, JL, Quinlan, AE, Peterson, GD, Wilkinson, C, Fünfgeld, H, McEvoy, D, Porter, L and Davoudi, S (2012) 'Planning theory and practice interacting traps: Resilience assessment of a pasture management system in northern Afghanistan, urban resilience: What does it mean in planning practice?, Resilience as a useful concept for climate change adaptation? The politics of resilience for planning: A cautionary note', *Planning Theory & Practice* 13 (2): 299–333.

Davis, R, Cook, D and Cohen, L (2005) 'A community resilience approach to reducing ethnic and racial disparities in health', *American Journal of Public Health* 95 (12): 2168–2173.

Dempsey, N, Bramley, G, Power, S and Brown, C (2009) 'The Social Dimension of Sustainable Development: Defining Urban Social Sustainability', *Sustainable Development* 19: 289–300.

Department of Health, Ministry of Public Health (2004) *The Health Impact Assessment for Healthy Public Policy: A Case Study of 'Garden City Project' Yala City, Thailand*, accessed January 2014 at: www.apho.org.uk/resource/item. aspx?RID=47674

Department of Sociology and Human Geography. University of Oslo website, posted 1 February 2011, accessed 1 July 2015 at: www.sv.uio.no/iss/english/ research/subjects/urban-development/

DFID (1999) *Sustainable Livelihoods Guidance Sheets. Department for International Development*, Government of the United Kingdom, accessed 2014 at: www.efls.ca/webresources/DFID_Sustainable_livelihoods_guidance_sheet.pdf

Dubois, J-L (2005) 'The Search for Socially Sustainable Development: Conceptual and methodological issues', Paper presented at the International Conference in Kyoto: Ethics, Economics and Law against injustice, Ristumeikan University, 28–30 October 2005.

Emery, M, Fey, S, Flora, C (2006) 'Using Community Capitals to Develop Assets for Positive Community Change', *CDP Practice Issue 13*, accessed on 22 December 2015 at: http://srdc.msstate.edu/fop/levelthree/trainarc/socialcapital/ communitycapitalstodevelopasset-emeryfeyflora2006.pdf

Engbersen, R and Sprinkhuizen, A (1997) *Nederland aan de monitor: het systematisch en periodiek volgen van maat schappelijke ontvikkelingen*, Utrecht: NIZW.

Erikson, K (1978) *Everything in Its Path: Destruction of Community in the Buffalo Creek Flood*, New York: Simon & Schuster.

Fagence, M (1977) *Citizen Participation in Planning*, Oxford: Pergamon.

Fataar, R and Petzer, B (2014) 'Cape Town's Anti-Apartheid Urban Plan: Reclaiming a City from a History of Hate', *Next City* website, 9th May 2014, accessed on 23 December 2015: http://nextcity.org/forefront/view/cape-towns-anti-apart heid-urban-plan

Ferlander, S (2007) 'The importance of different forms of social capital for health', *Acta Sociologica* 50: 115–128.

Ferrer, RA, and Klein, WMP (2015) 'Risk perceptions and health behaviour', *Current Opinion in Psychology* 5: 85–89.

Ferroni, M, Mateo, M, Payne, M (2008) *Development under Conditions of Inequality and Trust: Social Cohesion in Latin America*, IFPRI Discussion Paper 00777, Washington, DC: International Food Policy Research Institute.

Flora (2012) 'Surat: the not-so-little-city that could', *The Accidental Londoner* website/blog, accessed on 23 December 2015 at: www.theaccidentallondoner. com/2012/03/surat-not-so-little-city-that-could.html

Forrest, R and Kearns, A (2001) 'Social cohesion, social capital and the neighbourhood', *Urban Studies* 38 (12): 2125–2143.

Gehl, J (2010) *Cities for People*, Washington DC: Island Press.

Gehl, J (2006a) *New City Life*, Copenhagen: The Danish Architectural Press.

Gehl, J (2006b) *Life between Buildings: Using Public Space*, Copenhagen: The Danish Architectural Press.

Ghanekar, A, Desai, V, Desai, H, Kumar Rathi, S, Acharya, A, Khatri, K (2014) 'Building resilience to climate change and health: Can adolescents in urban slums be the answer?', *Asian Journal of Research in Social Sciences and Humanities* 4 (11): 1–15, accessed on 22 December 2015 at: http://uhcrc.org/sites/uhcrc.org/files/Research%20paper_adolescents%20perspective%20CC%20and%20health.pdf

Gillin, JL and Gillin, JP (1954) *Cultural Sociology: A Revision of an Introduction to Sociology*, New York: MacMillan.

Global Commission on the Economy and Climate (2014) *Better Growth, Better Climate: New Climate Economy 2014 Report*, Washington DC: World Resources Institute, accessed on 22 December 2015 at: http://newclimateeconomy.report/wp-content/uploads/2014/08/NCE_GlobalReport.pdf.

Goldstein, B (2009) 'Resilience to surprises through communicative planning', *Ecology and Society* 14 (20): article 33, accessed on 23 December 2015 at: www.ecologyandsociety.org/vol14/iss2/art33

Goodland, R (1995) 'The concept of environmental sustainability', *Annual Review of Ecology and Systematics* 26, 1–24. p. 3 (from Figure 1).

Goodyear, S (2014), 'How to Help the World's Cities Prepare for the Next Disaster: A Conversation with 100 Resilient Cities president Michael Berkowitz', *Citylab* website, accessed on 6 December 2015 at: www.citylab.com/politics/2014/09/how-to-help-the-worlds-cities-prepare-for-the-next-disaster/380808/

Govind, PJ and Verchick, RRM (2015) 'Natural disaster and climate change', in Alam, S, Atapattu, S, Gonzalez, CG and Razzaque, J (eds) *International Environmental Law and the Global South*. Cambridge: Cambridge University Press, 491–507.

Grootaert, C and van Bastelaer, T (2001) 'Understanding and Measuring Social Capital: A Synthesis of Findings and Recommendations from the Social Capital Initiative', Social Capital Initiative Working paper No. 24., The World Bank Social Development Family. Washington DC: World Bank, accessed on 22 December 2015 at: http://siteresources.worldbank.org/INTSOCIALCAPITAL/Resources/Social-Capital-Initiative-Working-Paper-Series/SCI-WPS-24.pdf

Hagerty, BMK, Lynch-Sauer, J, Patusky, KL, Bouwsema, M and Collier, P (1992) 'Sense of belonging: a vital mental health concept', *Archives of Psychiatric Nursing* VI (3): 172–177.

Helliwell, JF and Putnam, RD (2004) 'The social context of well-being', in *Philosophical Transactions of the Royal Society B: Biological Sciences* 359 (1449): 1435–1446.

Hernandez-Garcia, J (2013) *Public Space in Informal Settlements: The Barrios of Bogota*, Newcastle upon Tyne, UK: Cambridge Scholars Publishing.

Holden, M (2012) 'Urban policy engagement with social sustainability in Metro Vancouver', *Urban Studies* 49: 527–542.

Holling, CS (1973) 'Resilience and the stability of ecology systems', *Annual Review of Ecology and Systematics* 4: 1–23.

Holling, CS (1996) 'Engineering resileince versus ecological resilience', in: Schulze, PC (ed.), *Engineering Within Ecological Constraints*, Washington DC: National Academy Press, 31–44.

Hummon, D (1992) 'Community attachment: Local sentiment and a sense of place', in Altman, I and Low, S (eds), *Place Attachment*, New York: Plenum Press, 253–278.

Hyde, M, and Chavis, DM (2007) 'Sense of community and community building', in Cnaan RA and Milofsky C (eds), *Handbook of Community Movements and Local Organisations*, New York: Springer, 179–192.

IPCC (2014) *Climate Change 2014: Synthesis Report. Contribution of Working Groups I, II and III to the Fifth Assessment Report of the Intergovernmental Panel on Climate Change* [Core Writing Team, RK Pachauri and LA Meyer (eds)], Geneva, Switzerland, accessed 30 November 2015 at: www.ipcc.ch/report/ar5/syr/

ITDP (2017) *TOD Standard 3.0*. Accessed on 15 September 2017 at: www.itdp.org/library/standards-and-guides/tod3-0

Jabeen, H (2017) 'Gendered space and climate resilience in informal settlements in Khulna city, Bangladesh', unpublished paper. Bangladesh: Department of Architecture, BRAC University.

Jacobs, J (1961) *The Death and Life of Great American Cities*, New York: Random House.

James, H (2012) 'How citizens and urban design beat crime', article for *Lee Kuan Yew World City Prize* website, accessed on 6 December 2015 at: www.leekuanyewworldcityprize.com.sg/features_khayelitsha.htm

Jenson, J (2010) *Defining and Measuring Social Cohesion*, London: Commonwealth Secretariat and United Nations Research Institute for Sustainable Development, accessed on 23 December 2015 at: www.unrisd.org/80256B3C005BCCF9ch/170C271B7168CC30C12577D0004BA206?OpenDocument

Karuppannan, S and Sivam, A (2011) 'Social sustainability and neighbourhood design: an investigation of residents' satisfaction in Delhi', *Local Environment: The International Journal of Justice and Sustainability* 16 (9): 849–870.

Kasarda, JD and Janowitz, M (1974) 'Community attachment in mass society', *American Sociological Review* 39: 328–339.

Kearns, A and Forrest, R (2000) 'Social cohesion and multilevel urban governance', *Urban Studies* 37: 995–1017.

Kelly, J-F (2012) *Social Cities*, Melbourne: Grattan Institute, accessed on 22 December 2015 at: http://grattan.edu.au/report/social-cities/

King, R, Orloff, M, Virsilas, T and Pande, T (2017) 'Confronting the Urban Housing Crisis in the Global South: Adequate, Secure, and Affordable Housing', Working Paper chapter in *World Resources Report: Towards a More Equal City*, World Resources Institute, at: www.citesforall.org

King, R and Rathi, S (2010), 'Urban Infrastructure and Climate Change in India: Constructing Environmentally Sustainable Cities', background paper prepared for *Report of High-Powered Committee on Urban Infrastructure*, Isher Ahluwalia, chair. Delhi: National Institute of Urban Affairs.

King, S (1983) *Co-Design: A Process of Design Participation*, New York: Van Nostrand Reinhold.

Klinenberg, E (2013) 'Adaptation: How can cities be "climate proofed"?', *Dept of Urban Planning. The New Yorker Digital edition*, 7 January 2013, accessed on 22 December 2015 at: www.newyorker.com/magazine/2013/01/07/adaptation-2

Konig, J (2002) *Social Sustainability in a Globalizing World: Context, Theory and Methodology Explored*, The Hague: UNESCO, accessed on 22 December 2015 at: http://portal.unesco.org/shs/fr/files/7596/11120888871moreonmost.pdf/mor eonmost.pdf#page=61

Kohlhepp, D (2012) *The Real Estate Development Matrix*, paper presented at the American Real Estate Society Meetings, St Petersburg, Florida, April 21 2012, accessed on 6 December 2015 at: www.ccimef.org/pdf/2012-299.The-Real-Estate-Development-Matrix.4-21-12.pdf

Krishan, A and Shrader, E (1999) *World Bank Social Capital Assessment Tool*, prepared for the Conference on Social Capital and Poverty Reduction, The World Bank Washington, DC June 22–24, 1999, accessed on 21 December 2015 at: http://siteresources.worldbank.org/INTSOCIALCAPITAL/Resources/Social-Capital-Assessment-Tool–SOCAT-/sciwp22.pdf

La Grow SJ (2010) 'Orientation to Place', in: Stone, JH and Blouin, M (eds) *International Encyclopedia of Rehabilitation*, accessed on 23 December 2015 at: http://cirrie.buffalo.edu/encyclopedia/en/article/3/

Lang, J (1994) *Urban Design: The American Experience*, New York: John Wiley & Sons.

Lanzafame, F and Quartesan, A (2009) *Downtown Poverty, Methods of analysis and interventions – A sourcebook for practitioners*, Inter-American Development Bank, Washington DC, accessed on 6 December 2015 at: www.iadb.org/intal/intalcdi/PE/2009/04190a01.pdf

Laverack, G (2001) 'An identification and interpretation of the organizational aspects of community empowerment', *Community Development Journal* 36 (2): 134–145.

Lee MR and Blanchard T C (2012) 'Community attachment and negative affective states in the context of the BP Deepwater Horizon disaster', *American Behavioural Scientist* 56 (24): 24–47.

Lench, HC, Darbor, KE and Berg, LA (2013) 'Functional perspectives on emotion, behavior, and cognition', *Behavioral Sciences* 3 (4): 536–540.

Littig, B and Greissler, E (2005) 'Social sustainability: a catchword between political pragmatism and social theory', *International Journal of Sustainable Development* 8 (12): 65–79.

Loftland, LH (1989) 'Social life in the public realm: a review', *Journal of Contemporary Ethnography* 17 (4): 453–482.

Low, SM and Altman, I (1992) 'Place attachment: a conceptual inquiry', in: Altman, I and Low, SM (eds), *Place Attachment*, New York: Plenum Press, 1–12.

McAslan, A (2010) *Community Resilience: Understanding the Concept and its Application*. Australia: Torrens Resilience Institute, accessed on 22 December 2015 at: http://sustainablecommunitiessa.files.wordpress.com/2011/06/community-resilience-from-torrens-institute.pdf

McKenzie, S (2004) *Social Sustainability: Towards some Definitions*, Magill, South Australia: Hawke Research Institute, University of South Australia, 1–29.

Magee, L, Scerri, A and James, P (2012) 'Measuring social sustainability: a community-centred approach', *Applied Research in Quality of Life* 7 (3): 239–261, accessed on 22 December 2015 at: www.springerlink.com.libproxy.ucl.ac. uk/content/6887603286343817/abstract/

Magis, K (2010) 'Community resilience: an indicator of social sustainability', *Society and Natural Resources: An International Journal* 23 (5): 402–426.

Maida, CA (2007) *Sustainability and Communities of Place*, New York: Berghahn.

Martin-Breen, P and Anderies, JM (2011) *Resilience: A Literature Review*, Bellagio Initiative, Brighton: IDS, accessed on 6 December 2015 at: http://opendocs.ids. ac.uk/opendocs/handle/123456789/3692#.VmOFQ7_-oWc

Martikainen, P, Bartley, M and Lahelma, E (2002) 'Psychosocial determinants of health in social epidemiology', *International Journal of Epidemiology* 31 (6): 1091–1093.

Mitlin, D and Thompson, J (1995) 'Participatory approaches in urban areas: strengthening civil society or reinforcing the status quo,' *Environment and Urbanization* 7 (1): 231–250.

Morgan, DHJ (2005) 'Revisiting communities in Britain', *The Sociological Review* 53 (4): 641–657.

Mumford, L (1954) 'The neighborhood and the neighborhood unit', *The Town Planning Review* 24 (4): 256–270.

Murphy, K (2012) 'The social pillar of sustainable development: a literature review and framework for policy analysis', *Sustainability: Science, Practice and Policy* 8 (1): 15–29.

Norris, F, Stevens, S, Pfefferbaum, B, Wyche, K and Pfefferbaum, R (2008) 'Community resilience as a metaphor, theory, set of capacities, and strategy for disaster readiness', *American Journal of Community Psychology* 41 (1–2): 1573–2770.

Nutbeam, E and Harris, E (2004) 'Chapter 3: Theories on change in communities and communal action for health', in: *Theory in a Nutshell* (2nd edn), Sydney: McGraw Hill, 10–24.

OECD (1997) *Beyond 2000: The New Social Policy Agenda*, Paris: OECD.

OECD (2001) *The Well-being of Nations: The Role of Human and Social Capital*, Paris: OECD.

OECD (2006) *Competitive Cities in the Global Economy*, OECD Territorial Reviews, Paris: OECD.

OECD (n.d.) 'Stories of Empowerment Violence Prevention and Empowerment in the Township of Khayelitsha, South Africa', accessed on 23 December 2015 at: www.oecd.org/dac/povertyreduction/48869536.pdf

Oishi, S, Sherman, GD, Rothman, AJ, Snyder, M, Su, J, Zehm, K, Hertel, AW, and Hope Gonzales, M (2007) 'The socioecological model of procommunity action: the benefits of residential stability', *Journal of Personality and Social Psychology* 95 (3): 831–844.

Pahl, R (2005) 'Are all communities communities in the mind?', *The Sociological Review* 53 (4): 621–640.

Pharoah, R, Norman, W and Hale, T (2007) *Sirocco Site: Community Consultation*, London: ESRO (Ethnographic Social Research).

Polese, M and Stren, R (2000) *The Social Sustainability of Cities: Diversity and the Management of Change*, Toronto: University of Toronto Press.

Portes, A (1998) 'Social capital: Its origins and applications in modern sociology', *Annual Review of Sociology* 24 (1): 24.

Putnam, R (1993) *Making Democracy Work: Civic Traditions in Modern Italy*, Princeton, NJ: Princeton University Press.

Putnam RD (2000) *Bowling Alone: The Collapse and Revival of American Community*, New York: Simon & Schuster.

Quigley, R, den Broeder, L, Furu, P, Bond, A, Cave, B and Bos, R (2006) *Health Impact Assessment International Best Practice Principles*. Special Publication Serious No. 5. Fargo, USA: International Association for Impact Assessment.

Ria, A (2009) *Christchurch Transport Interchange: Health Impact Assessment 2007/08 – 2008/09*. Hui Facilitation and Maori Work Stream Report Writing. Report Prepared for Canterbury DHB.

Rowan, M and Streather, T (2011) 'Converting project risks to development opportunities through SIA enhancement measures: a practitioner perspective', *Impact Assessment and Project Appraisal* 29 (3): 217–230.

Sachs, I (1999) 'Social sustainability and whole development: Exploring the dimensions of sustainable development', in: Becker, E and Jahn, T (eds), *Sustainability and the Social Sciences: A Cross-disciplinary Approach to Integrating Environmental Considerations into Theoretical Reorientation*, London: ZED Books.

Sanoff, H (2010) 'Democratic or participatory design: Introduction', in: *Democratic Design: Participation Case Studies in Urban and Small Town Environments*, Germany: VDM Verlag Dr. Muller.

Semenza, JC, March, TL and Bontempo, BD (2006) 'Community-initiated urban development: an ecological intervention', *Journal of Urban Health: Bulletin of the New York Academy of Medicine* 84 (10): 8–20.

Serageldin, I (1996) *Sustainability and the Wealth of Nations: First Steps in an Ongoing Journey*, Environmentally sustainable development studies and monographs series; no. 5*ESSD Environmentally & Socially Sustainable Development Work in Progress. Washington, DC: The World Bank, accessed on 22 December 2015 at: http://documents.worldbank.org/curated/en/1996/07/696375/sustainability-wealth-nations-first-steps-ongoing-journey

Sherrieb, K, Norris, FH, and Galea, S (2010) 'Measuring capacities for community resilience', *Social Indicators Research* 99: 227–247.

Society of Practitioners of Health Impact Assessment (USA) Mental Health in HIA Working Group (2013) *Mental Health Definitions for Health Impact Assessment (HIA)*.

Spokane, AR, Mori, Y and Martinez, F (2012) 'Considerations in designing transitional communities housing arrays following disasters: Social vulnerability', *Environment and Behaviour* 45: 887–911, accessed on 22 December 2015 at: http://eab.sagepub.com/content/45/7/887

Stren, R and Polese, M (2000) *The Social Sustainability of Cities: Diversity and the Management of Change*, Toronto: University of Toronto Press.

Suzuki, H, Cervero, R and Iuchi, K (2013) *Transforming Cities with Transit*, Washington DC: World Bank.

Talen, E (1999) 'Sense of community and neighbourhood form: an assessment of the social doctrine of New Urbanism', *Urban Studies* 36 (8): 1361–1379.

Talen, E (2000) 'New Urbanism and the culture of criticism', *Urban Geography*, 21 (4): 318–341.

Thornley, L, Ball, J, Signal, L, Lawson-Te Aho, K and Rawson, E (2013) *Building Community Resilience: Learning from the Canterbury Earthquakes*, Report prepared for Health Research Council and Canterbury Medical Research Foundation, Christchurch, accessed on 6 December 2015 at: www.quigleyandwatts.co.nz/research-and-analysis/Building_Community_Resilience_report-March_2013.pdf?final2

Thornley, L, Ball, J, Signal, L, Lawson-Te Aho, K, Rawson, E (2014) 'Building community resilience: learning from the Canterbury earthquakes', *New Zealand Journal of Social Sciences* 10 (1): 23–35.

Thwaites, T (2015) 'UN Goals: Our cities hold the key to a sustainable future', *The Age*, accessed on December 10 2015 at: www.theage.com.au/comment/un-goals-our-cities-hold-the-key-to-a-sustainable-future-20150925-gjuv13.html

Tönnies, F (1887) *Community and Society*, New York: Harper Torchbooks.

Tokman, VE (2007) 'The informal economy, insecurity, and social cohesion in Latin America', *International Labour Review* 146 (1–2): 81–107.

Trentelman, CK (2009) 'Place attachment and community attachment: a primer grounded in the lived experience of a community sociologist', *Society and Natural Resources* 22 (3): 191–210.

United Nations (2005) *World Urbanization Prospects: The 2005 Revision*, accessed on 4 January 2016 at: www.un.org/esa/population/publications/WUP2005/2005wup.htm

United Nations Human Settlements Programme (UN-HABITAT) (2010), *State of the World's Cities 2010/2011: Bridging the Urban Divide*, London: Earthscan, accessed on 27 January 2016 at: http://mirror.unhabitat.org/pmss/listItemDetails.aspx?publicationID=2917

United Nations Human Settlements Programme (UNHABITAT) (2016) *State of the World's Cities 2016: Urbanization and Developmemnt*. Accessed 4 January 2016 at https://unhabitat.org/books/world-cities-report/

United Nations, Dept of Economic and Social Affairs, Population Division (2014), *World Urbanization Prospects: The 2014 Revision, Highlights* (ST/ESA/SER.A/352), accessed on 26 January 2016 at: http://esa.un.org/unpd/wup/Highlights/WUP2014-Highlights.pdf

United States Environmental Protection Agency (EPA), United States National Environmental Policy Act of 1969, EPA website, accessed 15 December 2015 at: www.epa.gov/sustainability/learn-about-sustainability

United States President's Council on Sustainable Development (1996) *Sustainable America: A New Consensus for the Prosperity, Opportunity and a Healthy*

Environment for the Future, accessed on 3 January 2016 at: http://clinton2.nara. gov/PCSD/Publications/TF_Reports/amer-top.html

Uphoff, N (2000) 'Understanding social capital: Learning from the analysis and experience of participation', in: Dasgupta, P and Serageldin, I (eds), *Social Capital: A Multifaceted Perspective*, Washington, DC: The World Bank, 215–249, accessed on 6 December 2015 at: www-wds.worldbank.org/external/default/ WDSContentServer/WDSP/IB/1999/11/19/000094946_99110505361324/Ren dered/PDF/multi_page.pdf

Vanclay, F (2002) 'Conceptualising social impacts', *Environmental Impact Assessment Review* 22: 183–211.

Vanclay, F (2008) 'Place matters', in: Vanclay, F, Higgins, M, Blackshaw, M (eds), *Making Sense of Place: Exploring Concepts and Expressions of Place through Different Senses and Lenses*, Canberra: National Museum of Australia, 3–11.

Vanclay, F, Esteves, AM, Aucamp, I, Franks, DM (2015) *Social Impact Assessment: Guidance for Assessing and Managing the Social Impacts of Projects*, Report for International Association of Impact Assessment, 98 pages, accessed on 6 December 2015 at: www.iaia.org/pdf/IAIA%202015%20Social%20Impact %20Assessment%20guidance%20document.pdf

Violence Prevention through Urban Upgrading website (n.d.), accessed 2014–2015 at: www.vpuu.org.za/index2.php and 'Baseline Survey Short Description', available at: www.vpuu.org.za/_files/pages/Baseline_Survey_Short_description.pdf

WCED (1987) *Our Common Future*. United Nations, accessed in2014 at: http:// conspect.nl/pdf/Our_Common_Future-Brundtland_Report_1987.pdf

Webb, M (1990) *The City Square*, New York: Watson-Guptill Publications.

Weingaertner, C and Moberg, A (2011) 'Exploring social sustainability: Learning from perspectives on urban development and companies and products', *Sustainable Development* 22 (2): 122–133.

Whyte, WH (1980) *The Social Life of Small Urban Spaces*, Washington, DC: The Conservation Foundation.

Wilhelm, M (2011a) 'Chapter 5: The role of community resilience in adapting to climate change: The urban poor in Jakarta, Indonesia', in: Otto-Zimmerman, K (ed.), *Resilient Cities: Cities and Adaptation to Climate Change Proceedings of the Global Forum 2010, Local Sustainability*, Berlin: Springer.

Wilhelm, M (2011b) 'Approaching disaster vulnerability in a megacity: Community resilience to flooding in two kampungs in Jakarta'. Unpublished Doctoral Dissertation, Achern: University of Passau, accessed on 22 December 2015 at: d-nb.info/1027610234/34

Williams, A and Kitchen, P (2012) 'Sense of place and health in Hamilton, Ontario: a case study', *Social Indicators Research* 108 (2): 257–276.

Williams, DR and Vaske, JJ (2003) 'The measurement of place attachment: Validity and generalizability of a psychometric approach', *Forest Science* 49: 830–840.

Williamson, T (2017) 'Rio's favelas: the power of informal urbanism', in *Perspectica* 50: Urban Divides. 213–228.

Woodcraft, S (2012) 'Social sustainability and new communities: Moving from concept to practice in the UK', *Procedia – Social and Behavioural Sciences* 68: 29–42.

Woodcraft, S, Bacon, N, Caistor-Arendar, L and Hackett, T with Sir Peter Hall (2011) *Design for Social Sustainability: A framework for creating thriving new communities*. London: Social Life, accessed on 23 December 2015 at: www.social-life.co/media/files/DESIGN_FOR_SOCIAL_SUSTAINABILITY_3.pdf

Woolcock, W and Narayan, D (2000) 'Social capital: Implications for development theory, research and policy', *The World Bank Research Observer* 1 (15): 225–249.

World Bank (2014) 'Chapter 4: Cohesive and connected communities create resilience', *World Bank Development Report* (WDR), Washington DC: World Bank, 139-163, accessed on 6 December 2015 at: http://siteresources.worldbank.org/EXTNWDR2013/Resources/8258024-1352909193861/8936935-1356011448215/8986901-1380046989056/WDR-2014_Complete_Report.pdf

World Bank (2013) *Brief: Social Inclusion*, August 15, 2013, accessed 3 January 2016 at: www.worldbank.org/en/topic/socialdevelopment/brief/social-inclusion

World Bank (2011) *Economics of Adaptation to Climate Change*, accessed on 23 December 2015 at: www-wds.worldbank.org/external/default/WDSContentServer/WDSP/IB/2012/06/27/000425970_20120627163039/Rendered/PDF/702670ESW0P10800EACCSynthesisReport.pdf

World Bank (2010) *Cities and Climate Change: An Urgent Agenda*. The World Bank Urban Development Series Knowledge Papers, Volume 10 (especially Part II), Washington DC: World Bank, accessed on 6 December 2015 at: http://siteresources.worldbank.org/INTUWM/Resources/340232-1205330656272/CitiesandClimateChange.pdf

WHO (n.d.) accessed 26 January 2016 at: www.who.int/gho/urban_health/situation_trends/urban_population_growth_text/en/

World Resources Institute (2011) *World Resources Report 2010-2011, Decision Making in a Changing Climate: Adaptation Challenges and Choices*, accessed on 23 December 2015 at: http://pdf.wri.org/world_resources_report_2010-2011.pdf

Wrong, D (1994) *The Problem of Social Order: What Unites and Divides Society*, London: Free Press/Maxwell MacMillan.

Yuval-Davis, Nira (2006) 'Belonging and the politics of belonging', *Patterns of Prejudice* 40 (3): 197–214.

Zautra, A, Hall, J and Murray, K (2008) 'Community development and community resilience: an integrative approach', *Community Development* 39 (3): 130–147.

Zetter, R, Griffiths, D, Sigona, N, Flynn, D, Tauhid, P and Benyon, R (2006) *Immigration, Social Cohesion, and Social Capital: What are the Links*? London: Joseph Rowntree Foundation, accessed on 23 December 2015 at: www.jrf.org.uk/file/37076/download?token=VORkSS2P

Index

Printed in Great Britain
by Amazon

54929181R00119